The Word Among Us

JESUS 365

A DAILY INVITATION TO RENEW YOUR SPIRIT

Edited by Lucy Scholand

the WORD
among us®
press

Copyright © 2020 The Word Among Us.
All rights reserved.

Published by The Word Among Us Press
7115 Guilford Drive, Suite 100
Frederick, Maryland 21704
wau.org

24 23 22 21 20   1 2 3 4 5

ISBN: 978-1-59325-515-2 eISBN: 978-1-59325-517-6

Design by Suzanne Earl

Made and printed in the United States of America

Library of Congress Control Number: 2020911641

ACKNOWLEDGMENTS

Our tremendous gratitude to Terry Griesenauer and Missy Lowrey who came to us with the idea for this book. Terry and Missy experienced a deepening love for the Lord through *The Word Among Us* meditations and wanted to give others the same transformational opportunity. We are grateful for their support, wisdom, and guidance, from conception through completion.

Thank you to Lucy Scholand, a gifted editor who worked diligently and faithfully to bring these meditations to you!

CONTENTS

INTRODUCTION

The book you are holding in your hands is not your ordinary devotional. In fact, you could say it was thirty-nine years in the making. That's because the meditations in this book have been adapted from *The Word Among Us*, a devotional magazine that began publication in 1981.

The Word Among Us arose from the experience of a number of people, both lay and ordained, whose lives were touched by the Holy Spirit and who wanted to help other people come to know Christ in a deeper way. Many of these people no longer work on the magazine, but their influence remains with us—the "next generation" who learned from them and continue to carry on their mission. None of us are experts. We're not celebrated authors, seasoned preachers, or learned theologians. But that's the point: like our founders, we are sharing something that we are convinced is for everyone.

You'll notice that the daily meditations in this book are rooted in the Scriptures. That's because we believe that God wants to speak to us in his word—not just generally, but personally and individually. He wants to speak to the deepest desires of our hearts: our hopes and dreams, our fears and anxieties. He wants to give us guidance for our lives, and he wants to teach us how to love one another as Jesus loves us.

The Spirit wants to make it feel as if God is speaking directly to us as we read the Bible—because he is.

The Bible isn't meant to just be read; it's meant to be *prayed*. So every day when you open this book, begin by inviting the Holy Spirit to be with you. Read that day's Scripture passage slowly. Sit with it. Mull it over. Then read the meditation just as prayerfully. Ask the Holy Spirit to help you see how it applies to your life. See if there is a message God wants you to take with you into your day. It's that simple, but it can make a world of difference.

Jesus promised to be with us "always, until the end of the age" (Matthew 28:20). That means 365 days a year. It's our prayer that this book will help you come to know him better each and every day.

The Editorial Team of *The Word Among Us*

January

GOD MADE ME
FOR HIMSELF

January 1

In the beginning, . . . God created the
heavens and the earth. (Genesis 1:1)

Who is God? Here at the very start of the Bible, we see that God just plain is. He created the entire universe and everything in it out of sheer nothingness. He is Lord over all creation. And we are the crown of his creation, the culmination of all that he made, for "God created mankind in his image" (Genesis 1:27).

Since God created everything, we can be sure that he has more than enough power to work in our lives today. And God the Creator loves each of us as well: "God looked at everything he had made, and found it very good" (Genesis 1:31).

Every day we can place our hope in God our Creator, our Father. He has the power to save us. And because he loves us, he wants to save us!

Keep this central truth of who God is at the forefront of your mind today. Use it to help you trust that God is above every circumstance you will face.

"Father, we exalt you as the Creator of all that is. We believe that you love your creation and that you love each of us. Through your Spirit, help us to know you."

January 2

It is too little . . . for you to be my servant . . . ;
I will make you a light to the nations. (Isaiah 49:6)

What does God think when he looks at your expectations? Your vision is too narrow! Your dreams are too small! I want to do much more!

God sent the Messiah to be a light to all nations and to bring every person back to God. Jesus died to transform us, altering the very foundation of our lives.

God has a massive, exciting, glorious plan for your life! He wants to take your nature and fill it to overflowing with his grace. He wants to make you a light to the nations!

How wide and broad is God's plan to save the world! Today let him save and transform you. Let him bury the old you and raise a brand-new you to life.

"Lord, broaden my vision so I can perceive how you want to use me to build your kingdom!"

January 3

You formed my inmost being;
you knit me in my mother's womb. (Psalm 139:13)

Oh, how fearfully and wonderfully you are made! Thirty trillion cells, 206 bones, 650 muscles, and 79 internal organs work in unison. Your body's systems enable you to combat disease and take in nourishment.

Your arms, hands, and fingers allow you to touch, feel, and lift. Your legs carry you, your feet move you, and your toes stabilize you. Your brain empowers you to imagine, memorize, think, and choose.

At the apex of your being dwell your deepest desires—all your hopes and dreams—as well as your conscience, your ability to love, and the greatest gift: the capacity to have deep and eternal fellowship with Almighty God! When he "knit you" together, he set you apart to share in his goodness and his love.

How amazing God's creation is. And you are his masterpiece!

"Marvelous are your works, Lord! I am in awe over how much thought you put into creating me. I praise you and thank you for giving me life."

January 4

Ask now of the days of old . . . : Did anything so
great ever happen before? (Deuteronomy 4:32)

Moses urged the Israelites to recall what God had done. Why? So that they could see God's faithfulness, power, and compassion toward them—and believe in him more deeply. "Fix [it] in your hearts" (Deuteronomy 4:39), Moses pleaded.

One of the most amazing features God gave us is memory. As helpful as it is for everyday life, God has a much higher goal: he gave us this gift to help us know him. We can recall what he has said to us and reflect on what he has done in our lives and throughout history. This leads us to trust him and build a relationship with him.

God is always by our side, offering us his grace and giving us new strength for the life to which he calls us. So fix your mind on the Lord. Remember his goodness and faithfulness. Remember that you belong to him.

"Lord, I fix your words in my heart. Let me taste your good-ness today!"

January 5

Do not be terrified. (Luke 21:9)

Time and again, Jesus gave people a simple word of advice: "Do not be afraid," he told his disciples, "your Father is pleased to give you the kingdom" (Luke 12:32). At the Last Supper, he told them, "Do not let your hearts be troubled" (John 14:1).

Still today, in the face of every worry, Jesus offers reassuring words: "My Father is with you. I will never leave you or abandon you." You may encounter troubling things, but don't let them overwhelm you.

Wouldn't it be wonderful if we could enter into the new year holding fast to this simple phrase, "I will not be afraid!"?

Scripture promises that "everyone who calls on the name of the Lord will be saved" (Romans 10:13). Everyone who turns to him finds help in times of need. The Faithful One, our Shepherd and our Guardian, loves us. He tells us, "I am your shield" (Genesis 15:1).

Let the peace of Christ settle in your heart. Let that peace reveal to the people around you, "Do not be terrified."

"Father, I give you all my fears. Hold my hand in yours, and I will know your peace."

January 6

My word . . . shall not return to me empty. (Isaiah 55:11)

God tells us that his word goes out and accomplishes his will—and he's absolutely right! His word is creative. He said, "Let there be light" (Genesis 1:3), and there was light. So too with day and night, earth and sea, plants and animals, and human beings. When a word goes forth from God's mouth, it brings into being something that never was—life. It establishes in you what is lacking so that his life in you can flourish, so that your faith and your relationships can deepen.

God's word is also near to you. Perhaps you long for life, peace, joy, or patience; God's word can bring it about. He speaks words of healing and forgiveness over your life. His word can give you a new start, a permanent break with old habits.

Finally, God's word is alive! Jesus, the Word of God, became flesh, dwelt among us, and overcame death.

Nothing can conquer the word of God. So rejoice in that word today! Read it. Seek its guidance. Invite it into your life, and watch it bear fruit!

"Father, speak your word to me today. I long to be made alive with you."

January 7

Daniel was resolved not to defile himself. (Daniel 1:8)

Daniel and his companions were in exile and in a quandary: should they defile themselves with food that was offered to pagan gods or face punishment and death at the hands of a foreign king?

Often the Christian life can put us at odds with society. Do we continue to trust in God, or do we compromise in the hope of saving our reputation? We often know the right thing to do but need the courage to do it.

Turn to God in the silence of prayer or in the counsel of someone trustworthy and wise. Look to Scripture verses such as:

> Trust in the LORD with all your heart,
>> on your own intelligence do not rely;
> In all your ways be mindful of him,
>> and he will make straight your paths. (Proverbs 3:5-6)

Speak candidly about your weaknesses to the Father. Ask for his strength to help you move in the right direction. God will come with his angels to support you and keep you on the path of righteousness.

"Lord, I pray for your wisdom, clarity, and courage. Be my strength, and guide me on the way of life."

January 8

James, son of Zebedee, and John the brother of James, . . . sons of thunder. (Mark 3:17)

Nicknames can be descriptive and sometimes humorous, showing closeness and affection. In nicknaming James and John "sons of thunder," perhaps Jesus referred to their zeal, perhaps to their quick tempers (Luke 9:54). Jesus knew them well and loved them completely, warts and all.

Jesus knows us fully too. He sees our strengths and our love for him along with our weaknesses and shortcomings. He also sees how our checkered attributes might bear fruit for the kingdom of God.

Sometimes we overlook our flaws and emphasize our strengths; more often we focus on our weaknesses and feel inadequate. We miss the goodness that God has placed in us and dismiss our capacity for holiness.

Ponder what strengths God has given you and how he might use them. Realize too that, like James and John, you still need some refining. Don't worry, for the same God who worked patiently with the sons of thunder will work in you.

"Jesus, thank you for loving me. Use me to build your kingdom."

January 9

*I have much more to tell you, but you
cannot bear it now. (John 16:12)*

Jesus wasn't withholding information from his disciples.
He was giving them the opportunity to learn how to listen to the Holy Spirit, who was coming to live in them. He gives us this same Spirit.

God made us for the journey. He wants us to develop an ongoing relationship with him, learn how to listen to the Holy Spirit, and move closer to him every day. We don't need to know all the steps ahead of time. Our final destiny becomes clearer with each step we take.

Ask God what he wants from you today. Trust him enough to take the one step that lies before you, even if you can't see what is down the road. Day by day, step by step, he will tell you what you need to hear, and your relationship with him will deepen and become more fruitful.

"Lord Jesus, I want to grow in love for you and grow in confidence as I follow your voice."

January 10

Who has touched my clothes? (Mark 5:30)

Our prayer life might feel a little like a gumball dispenser: we put in the time, and God dispenses his grace. But God wants so much more for us; he wants a personal encounter between him and his beloved!

Look at the story of the hemorrhaging woman. It wasn't enough that she pushed through the crowds and touched Jesus to be healed. He wanted to touch her too! He wanted to look into her eyes, listen to her story, and assure her that her faith and trust in him saved her. It didn't matter that he was on his way to heal a rich man's daughter. This desperate woman mattered to him just as much as the important, influential Jairus did.

God wants to see us, to touch us, and to assure us of his love. We were made for union with him—and he longs for union with us!

Reach out for Jesus. Don't be surprised to find him turning and looking at you with love. Listen to his words of healing, encouragement, and direction. He loves spending time with you!

"Jesus, I believe that you are looking for me, wanting to speak to me and touch my heart. Here I am, Lord!"

January 11

God will wipe away every tear from their eyes.
(Revelation 7:17)

In terms of eternity, how important is what you are doing now? Focusing on the splendid plans God has for us can help us not get caught up in distractions or side roads that go nowhere. Consider, for example, what is in heaven and what is available here to speed us on our journey.

There, God shelters us with his presence. Here, we know his presence when we talk to him through prayer.

There, hunger and thirst are no more. Here, we can share what we have by contributing to our local food bank or give a drink of water to someone in Jesus' name.

There, God will wipe away every tear. Here, as we sit with a loved one in the last stages of cancer, we can wipe away tears ourselves as we minister Jesus' love.

Thanks to the redemption Jesus won for us, heaven is our inheritance, and every day brings us one step closer to our true home. Every day, God gives us countless opportunities to manifest the glory of heaven to the world. So enjoy the trip today, knowing that the destination is amazing!

"How glorious are your promises, O Lord! I revel in them today, even as I take up the call to work out my salvation in you."

January 12

Let justice surge like water. (Amos 5:24)

What is "surging" in your life? Perhaps it's conflict within your family, at your workplace, or in your congregation. Perhaps you're experiencing overwhelming grief, exuberant joy, or raging fury. Perhaps a global issue like sex trafficking or child slavery has you frustrated.

In all these situations, you can beg God for a productive way to channel your energies. Don't settle for sorrow or frustration! Sit in a quiet place with the Lord, and pour out your concerns freely. Then wait for his words or intuitions to well up in your heart.

God is with you, and he will shed light on your path. He will show you the wise course of justice in every situation.

"Thank you, Father, for the reality of your love. Show me how to channel that love in a way that glorifies you and helps build your kingdom."

January 13

I will never forsake you or abandon you. (Hebrews 13:5)

There are no loopholes or limitations to this promise from God. When things are complicated, confusing, or overwhelming, God is with us. Even when we don't "feel" his presence, he is still there, giving his grace.

Relying on this promise, you can push aside any fear that robs you of sleep. You can find a way to be generous even when finances are tight. You can endure the exhaustion of having two jobs, being a new mother, studying for exams, or juggling multiple projects and schedules. You can find peace and joy in the midst of it all, because you know that God is with you.

In whatever circumstances you find yourself, ask God, "Where are you right now?" He may surprise you with what he says about who he is and who you are to him. And he will calm your fears and give you the assurance that he can bear you up as you keep trying to be hospitable, generous, and loving.

"Father, where are you right now? Help me rest confidently in your strength and love."

January 14

A large number of people came to him. (Mark 3:8)

Everywhere Jesus went, people crowded around, eager to touch him, to hear what he had to say, and to experience miracles. Here Jesus took the practical step of getting into a boat, from which he could be heard by many without being trampled.

But Jesus never related just to a "crowd." He had eyes and ears and a heart for each individual in front of him. He touched a leper. He forgave a sinner. He answered a question. He focused on whoever stood before him.

Jesus loves the whole world. He bore the sins of all humanity and brings resurrection life to all. But he still wants to touch each person individually—every wounded soul, every broken heart, every man, woman, and child.

Jesus might find you in a large group or by yourself in some quiet place. He will find you—especially if you seek him.

"Jesus, thank you for knowing me and loving me so completely. I lift my face to you. Come and touch me to the very core of my being."

January 15

[He] rejoices greatly at the bridegroom's voice. (John 3:29)

The Gospel shows John the Baptist as a man of great passion but also of great humility—a man who was eager to meet the Messiah and then stand aside so that Jesus could take center stage. He saw the Lord, and his joy was complete.

John tells us that God's voice is the voice of a smiling, exuberant bridegroom on his wedding day. It's a voice that longs to whisper words of love to his bride. It's a voice of hope and love, a voice of tenderness and yearning, a voice that brings joy.

As we listen for the voice of Jesus in prayer, we will hear words of direction, words of comfort, words of wisdom, and even words of correction. These words will come in a voice of love, acceptance, and friendship.

Take time today to pray. Quiet your heart, open your Scriptures, and listen closely. The Bridegroom has something to say to you.

"Here I am, Lord, ready to hear your voice. Let your words of truth and love awaken my heart."

January 16

*David came dancing before the L*ORD *with abandon.*
(2 Samuel 6:14)

Do you ever feel like dancing before God in your prayer time? How about singing a song or marching around the room? Or then again, walking meditatively through a forest, delighting in God's gift of the created world?

You might let out a hearty laugh because the Lord has made you joyful. Or you might kneel before the Lord, saying the name of Jesus over and over.

Our prayer can take many forms. Traditional prayer has its place, but God also wants us to feel free to express ourselves. An unscripted expression of praise, love, or gratitude may help us break through to a deeper relationship with God.

Remember that God is your Father. He loves you as his very own child. He delights in seeing you come before him to love him and to express that love.

"Jesus, teach me to express my joy and worship. You are great, O Lord, and I take delight in you!"

January 17

Whoever comes to me will never hunger. (John 6:35)

The people who saw Jesus seemed ready enough to accept that he could multiply bread. But could he really give anyone who believed in him "eternal life" and "raise him [on] the last day" (John 6:40)? Maybe that was too much.

How easy it can be to box God into some narrow category. No matter what our images of him are, how much bigger and better God is! He is a Father of endless mercy who desires to welcome all his sons and daughters to his banquet. Not only that, but he wants to make us become like him and bring us to live with him forever.

Partaking in God's divine nature is the awesome destiny God has for you. He loves you so much that he offers you a share in the very mind and heart of the Father, Son, and Holy Spirit. You are called to share in God's glory with Christ, and to pray with the Holy Spirit in you. Your prayers can change the world—securing blessings for its leaders, disrupting evil, reducing suffering, bringing healing.

Believe in Christ! Move ahead with confidence in God and his loving plan.

"Father, thank you for calling me to be with you for eternity and to know you even now! Increase my confidence in you, and help me see you as you really are."

January 18

He calls his own sheep by name and leads them out.
(John 10:3)

Sheep know better than to follow a stranger's voice; in fact, Jesus speaks of sheep who have become so accustomed to their shepherd that they won't even acknowledge another person's voice. This is God's vision for all of us. He fashioned us with the capacity to hear his voice and to be formed by his word.

God gave us each a conscience, a gift that is more than a "sin gauge"—telling us how wrong or right a certain action is—but the place where we hear the Lord clearly and intimately. It is where we learn about ourselves, for there we hear our Father tell us who we really are.

Our conscience is a place of invitation to use our unique gifts to become God's messengers of grace and love: "Pray for that friend who lost his job"; "Give your daughter a call, and tell her that you love her." As we respond to these invitations, we will build God's kingdom on earth!

"Lord, help me be still, hear your voice, and walk in your love and grace."

January 19

Show us the Father, and that will be enough for us.
(John 14:8)

God made us with a built-in longing for him. It's a deep craving—so deep, in fact, that some of us don't even know it's there.

Can we really know him who stretched out the universe?

God's throne is in heaven, and we are on earth. His thoughts and his ways are high above ours. But the answer is yes. And we already do know him because we know Jesus!

As we seek Jesus, we can know the Father more deeply. We might find out something brand-new about him; he has a way of challenging our assumptions about things. Often he shows us something we already know—like how much he loves us or how glorious he is—and he lets us experience it in a deeper way.

What's amazing is that however close to God we have grown over the years, there's always more to learn. There's always more to experience.

So may the prayer of Philip echo in our hearts: "Show us the Father!"

"Lord Jesus, show me the Father in a deeper way."

28

January 20

Our Father in heaven,
hallowed be your name.
(Matthew 6:9)

The Lord's Prayer is just fifty-five words, which means you can recite it comfortably in less than twenty seconds. Have you ever wondered why this one prayer that Jesus taught us is so brief?

First, long prayers don't capture God's attention any better than short prayers. God is attentive to us because he loves us.

Second, the Lord's Prayer is easy to memorize. Jesus made it easy for anyone to learn this prayer by heart and carry it with them wherever they go.

Third, the Lord's Prayer creates space for listening. We pray the essentials, and we still have plenty of time to hear what the Lord wants to say and to let his words touch us. The best prayer times are like that.

Recite the Lord's Prayer slowly, dwelling on each phrase. God hears every word. What's more, he sees your heart. Thank him for giving you such a beautiful, simple prayer.

"Father, thank you for always listening. Help me open my eyes and ears to you."

January 21

He chose us in him, before the foundation of the world.
(Ephesians 1:4)

The Population Reference Bureau has estimated that approximately 108 billion people have lived on Earth. So can you imagine that before God created the world, in the midst of these 108 billion people, he knew you perfectly and chose you to be with him?

God's love for us is not generalized; it is personal and specific. He loves you for who you are. He loves you in the best way you can be loved.

Here's one way to ponder this amazing truth: read Ephesians 1, and wherever you see the word "us," substitute your name: "Blessed be the God and Father of our Lord Jesus Christ, who has blessed [your name] in Christ with every spiritual blessing in the heavens, as he chose [your name] in him, before the foundation of the world, to be holy and without blemish before him." Proclaim it out loud.

God loves you. Bask in that love today.

"Father, I am amazed to know that I am in your heart. Help me trust and rely on your personal love today and every day."

January 22

Their eyes were opened. (Matthew 9:30)

Isaiah predicted that "the eyes of the blind shall see" (29:18). Jesus fulfilled this prophecy by restoring sight to two blind men. We can have confidence when we pray, "Open our eyes to your presence, Lord. Help us to see!"

God has many ways of opening our eyes to who he is. Maybe we see his beauty in a flower garden. We sense his love in our new grandchild. We experience his joy in prayer.

God also opens our eyes to how we can act. He gives us solutions to dilemmas we face, inspires trust in his care for us and our loved ones, and even gives us compassion for and the ability to forgive those who have hurt us.

God is at work in your life. As you pay attention to the movements of the Spirit, you'll find your sense of hope and enthusiasm growing. Your faith will deepen, and you'll become more convinced that you are not alone.

God wants to open our eyes to his presence. Let's pray for this!

"Open my eyes, Lord. Help me to see!"

January 23

It was really for the sake of saving lives that God sent me here ahead of you. (Genesis 45:5)

If anyone had reason to break ties with his family and his God, Joseph did. His very own brothers had sold him into slavery! Yet in each new situation, Joseph looked to God for wisdom and strength. He lavished mercy on his brothers.

Surely God delighted in Joseph's faithfulness, but the story is really about God's faithfulness. God blessed all that Joseph did. God was even faithful to Joseph's brothers, saving them from famine and making them the fathers of the tribes of Israel.

God honors your faithfulness too. He sees your devotion in praying and serving and loving. He hears your prayers. And even when you're not faithful to him, he remains true to you.

God sometimes works behind the scenes, using your faithfulness to do more than you can imagine. He forges a way for you through whatever life brings. God has placed you where you are so that you can shine his light. You have the potential to help people find their way in this world . . . to find their way to the Lord! Do your best to be faithful, trusting that he will raise you up in his own time and way.

"Lord, help me to shine your light wherever I am."

January 24

I will never forget you. (Isaiah 49:15)

Isaiah uses the vocation of motherhood to illustrate God's love for us. Mothers reflect God's goodness, love, and devotion. They make countless sacrifices for their children, tirelessly protecting, nurturing, and forming them.

A mother comforting her child gives us a glimpse of the way God wants to comfort us. A mother worrying about choices her adult children are making can remind us of Jesus' words: "How many times I yearned to gather your children together as a hen gathers her brood under her wings!" (Luke 13:34). A mother giving her child advice can remind us of the psalmist's prayer, "Your hands made me and fashioned me; / give me understanding to learn your commandments" (Psalm 119:73).

Where would the world be without a mother's love?

It is even harder to imagine where we would be without our loving God.

So every time you think about your mother today, think about God. And rejoice in the love that surrounds you!

"Here I am, God, so grateful to be your child!"

January 25

If you are the Son of God. (Matthew 4:3)

Satan tried to get Jesus to question his identity by saying, "If you are the Son of God." But Jesus knew who he was. He clung to the word of God and stayed focused on his Father.

God wants you to stand firm on the truth just as Jesus did. He wants to convince you that you belong to him. He wants to make it clear that he is completely committed to you.

When the devil tries to knock you off your foundation, follow Jesus' example, and hold on to Scripture. You are God's child, born of the incorruptible seed of his own word (see 1 Peter 1:23). You are part of a chosen generation, a royal priesthood, a holy nation (see 2:9). You have been made alive with Jesus (see Ephesians 2:5) and set free from the law of sin and death (see Romans 8:2). Your heavenly Father will supply all your needs out of the riches of his own glory (see Philippians 4:19).

There are so many promises. Hold on to them! Believe them—and watch the devil flee!

"Thank you, Lord, for claiming me as your own!"

January 26

Jonah set out for Nineveh. (Jonah 3:3)

What a great prophet! Just kidding. Jonah ran away from God's first call to Nineveh, putting others at risk to save his own skin. He was unmerciful, self-pitying, and angry (see Jonah 1:3, 7; 4:1-3, 9). His full portrait is not a pretty picture!

Do you have your own unseemly moments of rebelling against God's plan?

If so, you can find at least two encouraging messages in Jonah's story.

First: *Just because you have faults and failings doesn't mean God can't work through you.* God isn't hampered by your limitations! He seeks your cooperation and holiness, but even if your motives are mixed, you can do beautiful things for God.

Second: *The work God gives you to do for the good of others is for your good too.* God wanted to save the Ninevites and the prophet as well! Likewise, when God calls you to something, he wants to give you more of his life, to flood your soul with his light and healing.

"Lord, what beautiful thing are you calling me to do for you today?"

January 27

He saved us and called us to a holy life. (2 Timothy 1:9)

God has called you, Paul tells Timothy, not because of what you can do or have done or will do, but "according to his own design" (2 Timothy 1:9). Of course, prayer and the good things we do are part of God's plan. But they are small parts of his greatest plan: to fill us with his divine life and usher us into the glory of heaven!

The call to holiness can be challenging, but not always. Sometimes it means gazing into the night sky and thinking about God's goodness. Sometimes it means enjoying a family gathering. At its heart, holiness is a deep assurance that God is with us, in prosperity or hardship, joy or struggle.

God has a plan to bring you to holiness. You will know some of the details in advance; others you will recognize only in retrospect. Each will cause you to grow in the love and knowledge of God: in holiness!

God wants you to be the best person you can be. What changes do you need to make in your life to do what Jesus would do?

"Father, thank you for the life you have called me to. Give me grace to trust you with the details as I say yes to you."

January 28

If you knew the gift of God. (John 4:10)

Jesus helped people see spiritual truths in their everyday lives. The Samaritan woman came to the well for water, and Jesus told her about living water, worship, and the promised Messiah. Then the disciples returned with lunch, and Jesus explained his mission and their part in it.

A man like us in all things but sin, Jesus knew the refreshment of a cup of cool water and the energy a good meal provides. He used these realities to teach us about God's power to refresh us and strengthen us for our journey.

We don't have to leave the physical world behind in order to develop a spiritual focus. God came to redeem this world and fill it with his divine power. He took on flesh in order to redeem our bodies and teach us to find his presence everywhere we look.

Listen for Jesus' voice as you take a drink of water, fold the laundry, drive to work, or cook a meal. He wants to tell you something good!

"Here I am, Lord, ready to hear your voice."

January 29

*I am sending you to . . . rebels who have
rebelled against me.* (Ezekiel 2:3)

Why would God go to the trouble of sending Ezekiel to
speak his message to people who didn't seem inclined
to listen? Because that's how lavish God is with his love!

God wants to speak to his people. He sent prophets, then
he sent his Son. Today, he continues to long to connect with
us. Even our less-than-ideal disposition doesn't change God's
desire to speak to us. He didn't tell his prophets or his Son to
avoid hard-hearted people. He didn't send them just to the
holy, the expectant, and the receptive.

Thank God that he is so persistent! Whether you are in a
particularly receptive place in your life or not inclined to listen to God talk to you about a certain area of your life, he
still wants to reach you and give you his love and guidance.

So keep your eyes open to God's messengers in your life
today! Let his word break into your heart and wash away
any obstacles.

*"Lord, I am amazed that even when I am preoccupied, you
keep speaking to me. Thank you for your relentless love."*

January 30

What is your name? (Genesis 32:28)

Your name defines you in a significant way. It identifies your family, and it might have an important meaning.

When Jacob realized that he was wrestling with an angel, he begged for a blessing. That blessing was expressed as a new name: "Israel," that is, "one who strives—or sticks—with God."

Each of us bears the name "Christian"; we are children of God who share in the life of the Trinity. We also have a special name that describes how our Father sees us and the calling he has on our lives: "To the victor I shall give . . . a new name, which no one knows except the one who receives it" (Revelation 2:17).

Bask in God's love for you. Ask him to give you a glimpse of how precious you are to him. Let him whisper to you the name he has chosen to express who you truly are. And when you face a new choice in life, take a decisive step in the direction of that God-given identity.

"Father, thank you for naming me your beloved. Give me the grace to grow into the way you see me."

January 31

Let us continually offer God a sacrifice of praise.
(Hebrews 13:15)

The Scriptures call us to praise God in every situation, both good and bad. Praising him helps us to take our attention off our hardships and put it on his good plan.

Praising God helps us find that place of "still waters" that refresh and restore us (Psalm 23:2). As we offer God our praise, we become more aware of his greatness, which in turn opens us up to his wisdom and direction. Praise helps us receive his love. It fills us with courage and peace.

We don't need to be behind closed doors to praise God. We can praise him in the car, on an elevator, or in the middle of a lunch break. Even while talking to a neighbor, we can lift our hearts to Jesus.

Let us continually praise God for who he is and what he has done for us!

"Father, thank you for your love and mercy. I praise you for holding me in the palm of your hand."

Notes

_____
_____
_____
_____
_____
_____
_____
_____
_____
_____
_____
_____
_____
_____
_____
_____
_____

February

GOD FORGIVES ME

February 1

*The woman whom you put here with me—she gave me
fruit from the tree, and so I ate it. (Genesis 3:12)*

Like Adam, we rarely like to face our weaknesses or deal
with the messes our sins cause. We often find it easier to
blame someone else, make excuses, and lie, all the while hid-
ing from God and from his mercy.

Jesus told us, "The truth will set you free" (John 8:32). No
matter how excruciating it can be to face our sin, surrender-
ing to God brings true freedom.

God didn't give Adam and Eve up to their sin. They may
not have asked for mercy, but he gave it to them anyway. He
clothed them and promised that one of their offspring would
deliver them (see Genesis 3:15). This is how merciful God is!

Let us follow the way of humility and repentance. There
we will find God's abundant mercy, grace, and love. He will
heal our wounds and change our hearts. All we have to do is
begin the journey back to God. If he spots us taking just one
or two steps toward him, he will run to meet us.

*"Father, I am in awe of your mercy and your commitment
to me. Help me look to you to receive grace and love today!"*

February 2

I will establish my covenant with you. (Genesis 9:11)

Destruction is never God's final word. Whatever "death" he allows in our lives is followed by the promise of new life. There's a rainbow after every storm.

Yes, God asks us to die to ourselves and resist temptation, but he asks this so that we can clear more space in our hearts for him and for his grace. He wants us to be more fully alive in Christ, more able to reveal his love to the people around us.

What hinders you from loving?

Is it gossip, overwork, resentment, or self-isolation? Give it up, and find life-giving substitutes. Take a walk with a friend. Find something upbuilding to say in every conversation. Ask the Holy Spirit to work creatively in you.

Keep your eyes on the prize: new life in Christ. It springs from every death to self that you embrace. It will lead you to the final prize: eternal life with Jesus.

"Here I am, Lord. I'm ready to die, that I might live in you!"

February 3

*I, the LORD, explore the mind
and test the heart. (Jeremiah 17:10)*

It is exciting to learn that God knows how we think and what we truly intend. But we might find it unsettling to come before the One who is all-knowing!

When God probes us, he is more like a surgeon working with a scalpel than a lumberjack wielding an ax. Gently he uncovers the thoughts and intentions of our hearts. Skillfully he separates doubts and defenses, hopes and desires, purposes and attitudes. Even when he reveals something that needs to change, he is quick to assure us of his love.

Let the Lord probe your mind and test your heart today. The light he shines on you is as warm as the sun. You are precious in his eyes! He gave his only Son so that you might have eternal life.

God extends his forgiveness in outrageous abundance. He is rich in truth but also in love. So open your heart to him today. Sit with him in prayer. He will do the rest.

"Father, look into my heart today, examine my thoughts, and strengthen me in your love."

February 4

For the sake of the ten, . . . I will not destroy it.
(Genesis 18:32)

Abraham sought God's mercy for the city of Sodom, whose citizens had committed many terrible crimes. God agreed to spare this city of thousands if as few as ten noble citizens could be found there. In the end he could spare only Lot and his family from destruction.

For those who turn their backs on God, there is an eventual limit to his mercy. But for those who turn to him, his mercy is unfathomable. Imagine wading into a vast ocean with waves that immediately wash away your sins. This is how your heavenly Father treats you the moment you turn to him and confess.

Dive into this ocean of mercy! Search the depths and heights of the Lord's tenderness and compassion. None of us deserve his love, but he delights in loving us!

"Thank you, Father, for your unbounded mercy! May your waves of love wash over me, cleansing my conscience and healing my wounded, sinful heart."

February 5

My heart is overwhelmed,
my pity is stirred. (Hosea 11:8)

The story of Hosea and Gomer is one of the most touching in Scripture. After a number of happy years together, Hosea is distressed to discover that Gomer has committed adultery. God tells him to forgive Gomer and welcome her back.

Then God tells Hosea that Israel, his beloved bride, treats him in the same way. Israel commits spiritual adultery by worshiping false gods and taking on pagan practices. God's love for his people remains. His "heart is overwhelmed," his "pity is stirred" (11:8). He "will not give vent to [his] blazing anger" (11:9).

Today, our false gods might be money, sexual indulgence, possessions, power, and status. Despite our attractions to these, God still loves us. His heart is compassionate toward the sinner. He but asks that we repent and receive the love pouring from his heart. In his presence we will find blessing.

Search your heart today. What false gods do you have to surrender and lay at the foot of the cross?

"Thank you, Lord, for never giving up on me. May I never lose sight of your love."

February 6

Isaac said, "Are you really my son Esau?"
And Jacob said, "I am." (Genesis 27:24)

Have you ever tried to wrestle the steering wheel of your life from God's hands?

God had promised Rebekah that Jacob would rule (see Genesis 25:23), but Rebekah couldn't wait for God's plan to develop. She and Jacob forgot that God is always in control. They took matters into their own hands and caused things to spiral out of control. Their deception of Isaac when he had become blind did a lot of damage. Rebekah had to send Jacob away, and she died without ever seeing him again. Jacob had to run for his life and spend many years in hard labor, always wondering if God or Esau would forgive him.

Years later God comforted Jacob through a dream filled with angels. And Jacob did live to be reconciled with Esau and carry on the covenant.

God has a plan; perhaps you want it to happen according to your timing. Stop and think. Trust in God. And if you do make mistakes, know that he is always ready to guide you, to forgive you, and to comfort you.

"Lord, help me feel peace knowing that you are in control of my life. Help me remember that even when I fall, I can come back to you."

February 7

[Uriah] ate and drank with David, who got him drunk.
(2 Samuel 11:13)

King David was caught. He had had an affair with the wife of one of his soldiers, and she was now pregnant. After a couple of botched attempts to cover up his sin with Bathsheba, he conspired to have Uriah killed in battle. David's transgressions piled up—adultery, lying, murder—and the result was a string of tragedies for him and his family.

Wouldn't it have been better if David had admitted his initial wrong and tried to make amends?

We know how hard this can be. We fear people's reactions to our wrongdoings, as well as facing our sin.

We never have to fear how God will react when we admit our sin. For one thing, he already knows what we have done! Beyond that, he has promised to forgive every sin, to heal wounded consciences, and to keep us in the palm of his hand.

Bring your sin to God and find forgiveness and restoration. He will give you courage to make things right. And you will be doing it with Jesus by your side.

"Holy Spirit, give me a repentant heart. Help me confess my sin and seek reconciliation and healing."

February 8

They shall beat their swords into plowshares. (Isaiah 2:4)

Isaiah used this image when he prophesied about the coming Messiah. He described a kingdom in which tools of war would be turned into instruments of life and peace.

We all have swords in our lives, "tools" that we use to hurt one another. Maybe we have a short temper. We might be moody and hold grudges, or maybe we're quick to insult or condemn. The Lord wants to take any biting words and teach us how to speak with compassion and understanding. He wants to take our anger and re-form it into mercy. He wants to help us make peace in our relationships.

We need to cooperate with the divine Blacksmith. We need to surrender our swords to him so that he can help us reshape them.

Don't be afraid to look for the swords in your life, the ways you have injured yourself or the people around you. God is ready to forgive, heal, and strengthen you. He can take every act of repentance, every prayer, every generous act, and fill it with his grace.

"Father, I surrender my swords to you. Thank you for forgiving and healing me."

February 9

Repent! (Matthew 3:2)

John the Baptist was Israel's biggest hit since Elijah. What drew crowds to this finger-pointing hermit dressed in animal skins? It was his call for repentance.

When John told his listeners to turn from sin, he also offered them restoration. God wanted to open the floodgates of heaven and shower them with his love, bringing them healing, reconciliation, and peace. We can hear this word and prepare our own hearts for Jesus.

Sin, fear, indifference, lack of compassion—these are obstacles to an intimate relationship with God. God wants to lead us out of guilt, alienation, and shame into joy and freedom. He stands ready to wash us clean and anoint us with his Spirit. Every time we turn to him and repent, he gives us another glimpse of his kingdom.

Take some time to examine your life in the light of God's truth and love. Where have you succeeded? Where have you failed? Ask God to walk with you and put you on the right path.

"Father, your mercy is without end. I praise you for sending your Son to redeem me and set me free."

February 10

If the wicked . . . do what is right and just,
they save their lives. (Ezekiel 18:27)

God offers a staggering deal to the wicked who repent. They will live, and their sins will be forgotten!

The pleasure of sin lasts only a short while; then comes emptiness, estrangement from God, wrecked relationships. Sin is an awful deal. God's way is different.

When we turn from sin, God forgives us and washes us clean. He wipes out all condemnation toward us (see Romans 8:1). He goes on to silence the accusing voice of the devil in our consciences (see Zechariah 3:2). Then he pours his love and grace into our hearts so that we can move forward with him (see Romans 5:5). We can be transformed into the image of Jesus!

God's offer stands for you today. Are there patterns of sin in your life? You can run to the Lord, confident that you'll receive mercy, forgiveness, grace, and life.

Now, that is an amazing deal!

"All praise and honor to you, Lord, for your promise of
mercy! Thank you for saving me from sin!"

February 11

While he was still a long way off, his father caught sight of him, and was filled with compassion. (Luke 15:20)

The prodigal son took his father's money and squandered it. He had nothing now but the ravages of his self-indulgence. He returned to his father's house cautiously, nervous and fearful about how his father would receive him.

His father was on the lookout for him. He ran to embrace this dirty, ragged young man. Without a word of reproach, he celebrated his son's return: he is alive!

What a moving image of our heavenly Father! He always keeps his eye out for us. No matter where we've wandered, he runs to embrace us, to treat us with mercy, and to rejoice at our return.

Jesus was no starry-eyed dreamer or spinner of fairy tales. He spoke divine truth. Your heavenly Father really does love you this much. He is always eagerly waiting for you to turn to him more deeply. Even now he runs toward you, longing to put his arms around you and welcome you home.

How do you react to his embrace?

"Father, I trust in your kindness and mercy. Thank you for opening your arms and welcoming me home!"

February 12

Courage, child, your sins are forgiven. (Matthew 9:2)

Have you ever said to yourself that you deserve something bad that has happened? Have you thought that you aren't worthy of any personal attention from God because of the ways you fall short of his call? Perhaps you find it easy to acknowledge that Jesus forgives but more difficult to forgive yourself.

Jesus told the paralytic that his sins were forgiven! Jesus showed that God is a Father who loves. God hadn't abandoned this poor man but was very much a part of his life, ready to work wonders in him.

Scripture is filled with proof that Jesus' forgiveness is boundless. All he asks is that we turn to him and humbly confess our sins. He tells us to take courage, because we are forgiven. We belong to him, and he is always with us.

Let Jesus call you "child" today. Let him assure you that your sins *are forgiven*. Then let him continue to heal your inner self.

"Jesus, thank you for your boundless mercy! Thank you that I can bring all my needs to you for healing. Lord, I am in awe of your love!"

February 13

Great and awesome God, you who keep your covenant
and show mercy toward those who love you.
(Daniel 9:4)

Awesome. Merciful. Covenant. This might seem like a strange way to begin a prayer of repentance. And yet here is Daniel, confidently proclaiming God's love before confessing his sins and the sins of his people.

How could he be so certain that God would forgive? Because time after time, God had shown Daniel how much he treasured him. He provided for his swift promotion in a Gentile kingdom. He saved him in the lions' den and from a conspiracy against him. Having experienced God's mercy so concretely, Daniel willingly came clean before the Lord.

Our heavenly Father is good and generous. Recall his goodness to you over the years. Surely you can trust that he is willing and able to forgive.

Proclaim God's mercy and love for you as you confess your sins to him: "To the Lord, our God, belong compassion and forgiveness" (Daniel 9:9).

"Lord, help me lay my sins at your feet so that I can know true freedom."

February 14

Come now, let us set things right,
says the LORD. (Isaiah 1:18)

Isaiah spoke the cry of God's heart. Come and be cleansed, he pleaded; come and receive healing, restoration, freedom.

In human suffering and war, in faithlessness and rebellion, in exile and slavery, God's call remains constant: Return to me. Let me forgive you and wash you clean.

You can come to the Lord every day and set things right. Quiet your heart, and listen closely. You will hear the Lord calling you, urging you, Come, let us set things right.

Before you go to bed, reflect on your thoughts and actions that day, and bring to the Lord any ways in which you have missed the mark. It is a freeing experience to clear the decks every evening. It can even help you get a good night's sleep!

God reaches out to you, offering a torrent of healing love and merciful grace. He seeks you and is always ready to heal and forgive.

"Father, I stand in wonder at your desire to welcome me home! Your love truly is amazing!"

February 15

Everyone who looks at a woman with lust has already committed adultery. (Matthew 5:28)

A single glance can lead you down the road of temptation. But your eyes can also help get you out of it.

If your neighbor's car makes you dissatisfied with your own, stirring a temptation to greed, turn your eyes from both cars and toward the poor—maybe that homeless man you see on the corner as you drive to work. If a movie star attracts your attention, shift your gaze to your spouse, remembering all the times he or she has stayed up late with a sick baby, worked extra hours so you can afford a vacation, or made your favorite meal.

No matter what situation you are in, turn your eyes to Jesus. Gaze at a cross, and see God's love for you. Look at what Jesus did for you, and let him show you his love and faithfulness again!

"Jesus, I give you everything that competes for my attention. When I struggle, help me lift my eyes to your cross."

February 16

I . . . brought you out of . . . the house of slavery.
(Exodus 20:2)

No one wants to be owned by someone else. We should have the same attitude toward slavery to sin. As St. Paul said, we were created to be free, and Jesus came to "set us free" (Galatians 5:1).

Do you want to experience freedom from a sinful habit? Here are two suggestions.

First, confess your sins each day in prayer. Believe in the promise of Scripture: "If we acknowledge our sins," God will "cleanse us from every wrongdoing" (1 John 1:9).

Second, pray for the strength to resist sin. Trust that God sees your efforts and blesses them with his own power, to help you say no when temptation arises.

Sanctification comes as we pray, confess our sins, and seek God's strength. Sin loses its power as we grow strong in our efforts to resist.

"Lord, I don't want to be a slave. Help me be free."

February 17

The kingdom of God is at hand. Repent,
and believe in the gospel. (Mark 1:15)

Jesus preaches good news: God loves you. He wants to heal you and give you peace. He is near, offering freedom to all who turn to him.

This is the heart of repentance. God's love desires to liberate us from demons, restore our spirits, and renew our minds. Because of Jesus' death and resurrection, we can live in freedom.

Approach the throne of grace boldly. Open your heart, and accept everything Jesus has won for you.

To start, you might sit quietly and tell God one thing that keeps you from him: one habitual sin, one weakness, or one fear that bars your access to him. Offer to trade that one thing for a taste of his love. Then wait for the Holy Spirit to speak to you.

Whatever happens, know that the Father is with you, ready to forgive and heal and free.

"Father, I want to live in freedom, so I come to you today repenting and seeking more of your love."

February 18

The last will be first, and the first will be last.
(Matthew 20:16)

Jesus tells a parable about a landowner who paid his workers the same no matter when they showed up. The kingdom of heaven is like this, he says: God's kindness is available to everyone who will receive it.

Now, why should someone who has done terrible evil be admitted to the same heaven as we are? After all, we have worked so hard to please the Lord!

Scripture reminds us that salvation "depends not upon a person's will or exertion, but upon God, who shows mercy" (Romans 9:16). Although good deeds should follow upon our conversion, they can't get us into heaven. At the same time, our sins can't keep us out of heaven if we confess them and turn to the Lord.

God wants to give you his mercy so that you can become a citizen of heaven. And he wants you to show that same mercy to everyone you meet—sinner and saint alike!

"Lord, your mercy is unfathomable. Teach me to look on everyone as being worthy of your love."

February 19

*Should you not have had pity on your fellow servant,
as I had pity on you? (Matthew 18:33)*

What would this world look like if we could love more, forgive more, have more empathy, and look at ourselves and each other the way God does?

Jesus tells the story of a man who was given the opportunity to do that. But after receiving pardon of an immense debt from his master, he turned around and acted out of a stingy heart toward someone else. Jesus teaches that anyone who has been forgiven much should love much.

Jesus gave all he possibly could when he died on the cross; there's no way we can repay him for this. The only right response is to embrace his love and let it make us into more merciful persons.

Let us stay mindful of all the sins for which God has forgiven us, and we will find our capacity to love expanding day by day!

"Thank you, Father, for treating me with so much love. May that love overflow in me, touching every person I encounter today."

February 20

He saw Levi . . . sitting at the customs post.
He said to him, "Follow me."
And he got up and followed him. (Mark 2:14)

Jesus looked deep into Levi's heart and saw someone worthy of love; he saw his value, his potential to do great things for the kingdom of God. And that look of love, that look of mercy and healing, made Levi want to respond.

Jesus didn't explain the entire plan he had for Levi with assurances like "Come with me so that you can travel around the world telling everyone about me, healing the sick, and writing a Gospel." He simply asked Levi to step away from the old and toward the new life he was offering.

No matter where you are in your faith life, Jesus is passing by today. He sees you; he knows your weaknesses and sins, your goodness and your potential. He invites you to step away from the old and toward the new, to follow him.

"Yes, Jesus, I will follow you. Help me step away from my weaknesses and toward you—and the full life you have in store for me."

February 21

By the standard by which you judge another you condemn
yourself, since you, the judge, do the very same things.
(Romans 2:1)

Paul could speak from experience. He once thought himself
righteous for observing the Law, but he learned that "all
have sinned and are deprived of the glory of God" (Romans
3:23). He urged people to look to God for their standard of
righteousness rather than to their own minds.

Are we all hopeless sinners destined for perdition? Not at
all! Paul's rationale for exposing our condition is to move us
toward Christ. We don't have to fix the problem ourselves.
We have a Savior who is powerful enough to lead us out of
the mire of sin and into a new life of grace.

The next time you are tempted to judge someone, go
straight to Jesus, and see what he's telling you about yourself. Is he pointing out some area of darkness in your heart?
Run into his light, and be embraced by his mercy!

"Lord, help me see everyone with your love, admit my own
weaknesses, and come to you for mercy."

February 22

It shall be a jubilee for you. (Leviticus 25:10)

The jubilee was a time when the land could rest, slaves be freed, and all debts be forgiven. It was a reminder of God's goodness and an invitation to treat each other with mercy.

We can say that we are living in a permanent state of jubilee because of Jesus' cross and resurrection. Forgiveness of sins, healing of soul and body, and God's mercy are available to every person in every land.

So why do many Christians live as if under a cloud? Where is our rejoicing?

Satan, a "liar" and a "thief" (John 8:44; 10:10), tries to whisper depressing and divisive thoughts to our minds, to make us lose sight of the grace and power that are available to us. Don't believe him!

Hold fast to the truths that are at the basis of our celebration. Jesus said, "Neither do I condemn you" (John 8:11). He assures us that nothing can separate us from his love (see Romans 8:39). God calls us his children (see 1 John 3:1).

So rejoice! The jubilee is ours.

"Lord, help me rejoice in you and in the power of your love."

February 23

*Praise the LORD, for he is good;
for his mercy endures forever. (Psalm 136:1)*

Lord, I give you thanks for your mercy and your faithfulness toward me. You love me, and I want to love you. You are loyal to me, and I strive to be loyal to you. You are merciful, faithful, loving, loyal, generous, and more, even when I am unfaithful.

Thank you, Lord, for being constant in love and always good to me. Your mercy endures forever!

Father, nothing I do causes your love to fade, for you are love, and you are unchanging. You are relentless in your pursuit of me. Your love paves the way for me to come back to you when I stray.

Thank you, mighty God, faithful and tireless, for your mercy endures forever!

Lord, I can love you because you first loved me. And when I am filled by that love, I can share it with the people around me. Thank you, Father, for your love endures forever!

"Thank you, generous, loving Father, for your kindness endures forever!"

February 24

For God all things are possible. (Matthew 19:26)

Why did Jesus exhort the young man to sell his possessions and give the money to the poor? Jesus wanted the man to trust in God, not in his wealth. "It is easier for a camel to pass through the eye of a needle than for one who is rich to enter the kingdom of God" (Matthew 19:24).

One tradition tells us that the "eye of a needle" was a small gate into Jerusalem. Camels had to go to their knees and crawl through, after being rid of any baggage that got in their way. To enter eternal life, we need to kneel in prayer and humility, acknowledging the sovereignty of Christ and the power of his salvation. Let's get rid of sinful baggage hindering our spiritual growth.

Only Jesus can bring us to holiness. Let's commit our lives to him anew, striving for the perfection that comes only by faith in him. Then we can know his power to save.

"Jesus, you are my only hope. I commit myself to you as Lord and Savior. Help me become the person you want me to be."

February 25

What are we to do? (Acts 2:37)

Peter's words shook his listeners deeply. Let them shake us too. Even if our guilt is hidden deep in our consciences, we all know that we have sinned. We stand guilty before God and are unable to remove that guilt on our own. What are we to do?

Once Peter explained who Jesus was, he talked about the good news God had promised centuries earlier: "Everyone shall be saved who calls on the name of the Lord" (Acts 2:21; see also Joel 3:5). Even the ones who crucified Jesus? Yes!

That's how gracious and generous God is. "The promise is made to you and to your children and to all those far off" (Acts 2:39). This is truly great news.

"What are we to do?" Peter answers his listeners—and us—quickly and confidently: repent! Turn to Jesus, confess your sins, and tell him you are sorry. Tell him you need his forgiveness. He is loving and merciful, and he will forgive you and set you free!

"Jesus, thank you for your promise. Come, Lord, and make me new."

February 26

I will cleanse them so that they will be my
people, and I will be their God. (Ezekiel 37:23)

This message from Ezekiel had a special sense of urgency.
Israel was in exile, banished from the Promised Land, and
God promised that he would bring them home. He wanted
to shepherd them, establish peace with them, and live with
them forever.

Are you in exile from the kingdom of God? Perhaps it is
an exile to drug and alcohol abuse or to the realm of anger
and resentment. Perhaps it is to the land of lying, cheating,
or stealing. Perhaps it is an exile to the nation of competi-
tion and pride.

If you are in exile, Ezekiel has a word for you: God wants
to bring you home! He is the only one powerful enough to
rescue you and plant you firmly in his kingdom.

No matter how deep your pain, how strong your sin, or
how stubborn your heart, God's hand is stretched toward
you. Reach out and grab it!

"Father, I believe that you are Lord and God. Come take me
by the hand, and lead me home!"

February 27

*If by the spirit you put to death the deeds of the body,
you will live. (Romans 8:13)*

Paul teaches us that holiness is the result of our cooperation with grace. We must do away with things that are opposed to the Lord and his way of life: "deeds of the body," like lying, stealing, or impurity; and attitudes of the mind, such as prejudice, resentments, judgments, and arrogance. Paul promises that as we put these things to death—as we turn away from them and fight their influence in our lives—we will become holy.

Paul urges us to do all this "by the Spirit." Human effort alone cannot bring holiness. We need the help that only God can give.

Turn to the Holy Spirit, and ask him for divine power to help you say no to sin and yes to Christ. Pay attention to his promptings—in your conscience, through Scripture, from your loved ones, and even in the thoughts that pop into your head.

The Spirit is on your side. He wants to make you holy!

*"Come, Holy Spirit, into my heart. Transform my thoughts,
intentions, and actions by your grace."*

February 28

May God go before me.
(Psalm 59:11)

Imagine driving down a crowded street with only the use of your rearview mirrors. The idea is laughable—and more than a bit dangerous. It just doesn't make sense to drive while looking backward.

We can apply this image to our spiritual lives. Most of the time, we need to be looking forward, not backward. Sure, we need to glance back to check for blind spots or to assess our progress—like when we review our day or learn from past mistakes. But overall, we need to be looking forward if we want to move forward.

We might think of mercy as a gift that deals with our past, and it is. Mercy indeed reaches back to cover our sins.

But the Hebrew word for mercy (*hesed*) can also mean "God's grace and favor"—his loving kindness toward us, which never fails. This expansive definition urges us to do more than seek God's mercy for our past sins and failings. Rather, we entrust our future to him as well.

God's mercy paves the way forward. So press forward, confident that God's mercy and grace will go ahead of you.

"Lord, I entrust my future to you."

February 29

Restore to me the gladness of your salvation.
(Psalm 51:14)

O Lord, I come before you humbly, acknowledging that my offenses have been an affront to your holiness, your justice, and your love. Have mercy on me, Lord!

O God, my thoughts, words, and actions have turned me away from your grace and your protection. My sins have affected my relationship with you and with my brothers and sisters. O Lord, in your loving compassion, blot out my sins!

Father, believing in you and trusting in your Son's death and resurrection, I have been redeemed. You throw my sins from me, as far as the east is from the west. Filled with confidence in your power and mercy, I confess my sins. Let me know healing and restoration.

Forgiven, I can stand straight again. I can breathe freely. I am strengthened through your grace to say no to temptation.

Thank you, Father, for the joy of being forgiven!

"Father, your love and mercy are unending! Inspired by your grace, I come to you now to be set free. Father, may I never forget you!"

Notes

March

JESUS, MY SAVIOR

March 1

*How much more will the blood of Christ . . . cleanse our
consciences from dead works to worship the living God.*
(Hebrews 9:14)

It's easy to recognize a child with a guilty conscience. He
avoids making eye contact and stays away from his parents and the "scene of the crime."

How often do you relate to God your Father like a guilty
child?

Maybe you walk around with your head down even after
you have confessed your sin. Maybe you do good deeds to try
to balance out the bad ones. But your efforts only obscure the
central issue: you have broken something that only God can fix.

By shedding his blood, Jesus has won forgiveness for us.
He has made us a new creation. His blood—his very life—
changes everything it touches, even us! We can walk in freedom
because we are children of God, forgiven and washed clean
by Jesus' blood.

Even more, he cleanses our consciences of any nagging sense
of guilt. He frees us to perform good deeds as a response of
gratitude, not as an attempt to please God.

What a loving God we have! What a merciful Savior!

"Jesus, thank you for your blood, poured out for me!"

March 2

Jesus came from Galilee to John at the Jordan.
(Matthew 3:13)

It's a big day! After thirty hidden years in Nazareth, Jesus the Messiah is on the move, going public with his mission to heal and save.

John the Baptist had a clear understanding of his mission: he was a herald preparing the way for someone "mightier" (Matthew 3:11). He was the best man and not the bridegroom. When the Messiah showed up, John was taken aback by Jesus' request to be baptized. "I need to be baptized by you, and yet you are coming to me?" (Matthew 3:14). As John baptizes him in the Jordan, Jesus is revealed as Savior, Suffering Servant, and "beloved Son" (Matthew 3:17).

Even in his confusion, John was humble enough to grasp that God's plan could be different from what he thought. At a word from Jesus, he accepted a role he never sought.

And who can fathom the depths of Jesus' humility? Out of love, the sinless One joins with sinners—with us—to show that he is truly "God with us."

"Who am I, Lord, that you would offer me so much? Jesus, teach me to be like you."

March 3

He shall bring forth justice to the nations. (Isaiah 42:1)

Christians have long seen the Suffering Servant in the Book of Isaiah as a foreshadowing of Jesus, the Messiah. The mission and the character of this servant give us insights into who Jesus is and why he suffered and died for us.

Key to the servant's mission is the call to bring justice to the world—God's justice, which combines tenacity and strength with gentleness and compassion. God wants to restore all of creation, including the weakest and hurting. We are the prisoners he sets free; we are the blind whose eyes he opens (see Isaiah 42:7); we are the poor to whom he speaks good news.

Jesus longs to restore you to your place as a beloved child of the Father. His eyes are fixed on the "bruised reeds" and "dimly burning" in your life (Isaiah 42:3).

He is mighty to save—to save you! So take your place in the drama of salvation.

"Lord, thank you for the salvation that you have won for me through your death and resurrection."

March 4

Come to me, all you who labor and are burdened,
and I will give you rest. (Matthew 11:28)

We have all kinds of reasons why we don't come to Jesus. Guilt or shame can keep us away. Or maybe we feel so busy that we don't make time for God. The myriad forms of media and entertainment can make it difficult to quiet our minds and settle into Jesus' presence. Or we might think, "I don't need anything from Jesus right now."

Jesus issues a compelling command, one with a promise attached. He still says, *Come! Come to me when you're feeling bad about yourself, when you think you're too busy, when you're distracted or depressed or anxious or lonely. Come even if you think you can do without me.*

Tell Jesus what's on your mind, even your sins. Then close your eyes and take a few deep breaths. You may not feel anything right away, but you can trust that he is pouring his blessings on you.

"Jesus, I need your rest, so I come to you to take on your yoke and learn from you."

March 5

Woe to you . . . (Luke 11:47)

Jesus had harsh words for the Pharisees and scribes who opposed him. He wasn't insulting them but rather expressing his sorrow at the wall their sin created between God and them. Jesus came to pardon and reconcile, and it broke his heart to see people turn their backs on his generous gift.

We might get angry about the wrong choices people make—especially when those choices hurt us in some way. But rather than condemn others, let us intercede. Prayer can give us a taste of the way Jesus mourns over sin. It can soften our hearts and wash away judgmental thoughts.

Don't be hard on yourself either! God loves you. He sent Jesus into the world not to condemn but to save (see John 3:17).

As we see Jesus' sadness over sin, we move closer to mercy. Let prayer draw us toward him, into the fullness of his life!

"Lord, give me a heart softened by sorrow, like yours. Let me love as you love."

March 6

I am the light of the world. (John 8:12)

Lord Jesus, you are light, and in you is no darkness! Your true light brings light to all people. It is constant and consistent amid the changing philosophies of our world. We can depend on you to never fade with time.

Lord, your brilliance has dispelled the darkness of sin, both in our hearts and in the world. Your light has shone forth like the sun's rays into every dark corner. You overcome sin and death with the light of your redemption!

All praise to you, Jesus, for illuminating our lives as we turn to you! Every day you shine your light on our way through your word in Scripture. Your light directs our feet and teaches us the way to go.

Lord, you have called us to be light to the world! We are reflections of your life. We are your beacons, manifesting your holiness, your joy, and your plan to all the world!

"Jesus, light of the world, shine in my life! Drive away the darkness of sin, convince me of your truth, guide my path, and enable me to shine your light to others!"

March 7

No one can take them out of my hand. (John 10:28)

What comforting words Jesus gives us! He is the one pursuing us, and he will not allow anyone to snatch us out of his hand. "My Father," Jesus says, "who has given them to me, is greater than all" (John 10:29).

God wants you to be surer of his love than of anything else in your life. That's because his love is the surest thing in all the world! You can live in joy and security, safe in the knowledge that God is on your side and that nothing can separate you from him.

Look at some of your fears. What makes you feel most vulnerable?

Give these areas over to God, and ask him to replace them with the joy and freedom that he has won for you. Let his greatness and his mercy put all your fears into perspective, so that you can live as his son or daughter, perfectly safe in your Father's hand!

"Dear Jesus, I am in awe of the way you pursue me. I give my fears over to you today; drive them out with your perfect love."

March 8

Why are you terrified, O you of little faith?
(Matthew 8:26)

The disciples didn't know that the boat they were in was the safest place on earth—because Jesus was with them. We see that in retrospect, but how often are we buffeted by waves of fear? Yes, the storms are real, but Jesus is with us, even if it appears that he's fast asleep.

What rocks your boat? Are you worried about your children? Are your finances overwhelming? Does a serious illness or disability threaten? Ask the Lord to speak to you through the storm.

"Lord, where are you? I am afraid and alone."

"I am here. Even if you can't see me or hear me, I am right beside you."

"I'm anxious, Lord."

"Fix your heart on me."

"But the storm is still here."

"That's okay. I am bigger than any storm. You can find peace in my presence."

Tell Jesus what you are dealing with. Ask him to give you his peace. Even if the circumstances don't change, they will lose their power to disturb you. Jesus is in your boat.

"Lord, grant me your peace."

March 9

They begged him to leave their district. (Matthew 8:34)

Jesus freed the Gadarenes from the grip of demons. So why weren't the people dancing for joy and begging Jesus to work more miracles for them? Perhaps it was seeing the pigs rush into the water and drown that scared them. This was just too strange.

Something unexpected might well happen when Jesus shows up. His power is out of our control. The same power that casts out demons may move us out of our comfort zones. Ask yourself, for example, "What if I ask Jesus to heal me, and he asks me to give up a grudge?"

One thing we can rely on: God is on our side! He loves us always, without reservation. He is merciful. He is unrelenting toward sin but overflowing in kindness and grace. He delights in us.

Ask Jesus to show you who he is and how he sees you. You will find joy and hope, dispelling all fear.

"Jesus, I want you to work in my life, but sometimes I'm afraid of what that will feel like. Let the reassurance of your love for me overflow so that I can trust in you."

March 10

*Why does your teacher eat with tax collectors
and sinners? (Matthew 9:11)*

Tax collectors enjoyed the benefits of Roman oppression.
The taxes they collected went toward funding this oppression and the desecration of God's holy nation. What's more,
tax collectors often used their military backing to cheat and
extort their neighbors for personal gain. No wonder tax collectors were hated!

Yet these are the people Jesus chose to spend time with.
He sat down with them even while they were still doing damage. It's not as if he accepted these people reluctantly and at
a socially acceptable distance. No, he strategically went after
Matthew, knowing that building a relationship with one tax
collector would open the door to many more.

Jesus recognized the true outcasts, the ones beyond pity.
Not only did he love them, but he made them part of his
team. He didn't look for perfection; he looked for comrades.

Have you considered how Jesus invites you to be part of
his team? The love Jesus showed to those tax collectors is
the same love he has for us. Praise God!

*"Lord, I am in awe of your mercy! Thank you for seeking
me out and inviting me to your table."*

March 11

*Peter got out of the boat and began to walk
on the water toward Jesus. (Matthew 14:29)*

During a storm on the sea, Jesus stood right in front of the apostles and told them, "It is I; do not be afraid" (Matthew 14:27). As Peter looked at Jesus, the storm seemed to fade. All that mattered was that Jesus was there, defying the laws of gravity and banishing fear.

Our hearts may be pulled this way and that by the waves around us: illness, financial concerns, relationship challenges, major decisions facing us. Jesus remains the one and only constant. He sits at God's right hand and has all power and authority. He loves us completely. Nothing catches him off guard.

Jesus tells us, "It is I; do not be afraid." Picture him before you, gazing at you in love and reaching out to help you.

"Jesus, I want to know you more. I want my heart to be so sure of you and your love that I can look above the waves in my life. Lord, you are worthy of my trust!"

March 12

He was transfigured before them. (Mark 9:2)

Jesus showed his disciples that he had come from God: he performed miracles, taught with authority, and revealed God's mercy. When he asked them, "Who do you say that I am?" Peter answered, "You are the Messiah" (Mark 8:29).

Still, the disciples' faith needed to grow. They would have to understand what kind of Messiah Jesus was, why he had to die, and how they were to take up the cross as well (see Mark 8:31-35). When Jesus was "transfigured before them," they realized that he wasn't just another prophet; he was God's Son! It also showed that even though Jesus had to die, he would rise to a glory beyond their imagining.

God was strengthening the disciples—and all of us as well. He gives us a glimpse of the glory that Jesus had before coming to earth, the glory that he now enjoys on his heavenly throne. And he reveals the glory that awaits each of us if we remain faithful to the Lord.

Accept Jesus' invitation to follow him. You will be changed "from glory to glory" (2 Corinthians 3:18).

"Here I am, Lord, ready to do your will. Fill me with your grace."

March 13

The greatest among you must be your servant.
(Matthew 23:11)

Some of the scribes and Pharisees of Jesus' day succumbed to the allure of elitism and forgot God's call to care for the poor, the widow, and the orphan. In contrast to them, Jesus set people free from whatever was burdening them. He released a woman from the burden of shame over her past sins (see Luke 7:36-50); called Zacchaeus, a despised tax collector, a treasured son of Abraham (see 19:1-10); and consoled two downhearted disciples on the road to Emmaus (see 24:13-35).

Is there a burden that you're carrying? Guilt? The pain of a wounded relationship? Powerlessness in the face of temptation?

Jesus became a man like us. He came to serve. He shared the joys and sorrows we experience. He carried the cross so that we might gain heaven. Surely he can help you!

Take what is burdening you, and bring it to the Lord. Nothing is too small—or too big—for him to handle. Tell him your concern, then listen quietly for his words of comfort, wisdom, and help.

"Jesus, I surrender to you."

March 14

Israel loved Joseph best of all his sons. (Genesis 37:3)

Many events of the Old Testament anticipate realities fully revealed in the New Testament. The story of Joseph, son of Jacob, gives us a stirring anticipation of Jesus.

Joseph and Jesus were both favored sons of loving fathers. Both experienced rejection from their own people. Both were sold for silver. Both were falsely accused and imprisoned. Both were unexpectedly exalted—Joseph to Pharaoh's throne and Jesus to the throne of God. And both provided salvation for the chosen people as well as the Gentiles around them. "Even though you meant harm to me," Joseph told his brothers, "God meant it for good" (Genesis 50:20).

The people, prophecies, and events in the Old Testament can help us come to a deeper grasp of the salvation that Jesus has won for us. Look for Jesus' "footprints" in the Old Testament, and you'll see how much God loves his people—including you.

Where do you see Jesus' footprints in your life today?

"Jesus, you are the Lord of history. Thank you for opening my eyes to your wonderful plan for our salvation!"

March 15

Follow me. (Matthew 9:9)

Imagine yourself in Matthew's shoes. You've heard about Jesus, a miracle worker who might be the Messiah. He opens the eyes of the blind, speaks about God's forgiveness, and treats the poor and outcast with kindness. Now he stands before you.

He says, "Follow me." You're caught off guard: Why would he say this to me? I've never even met him before. What about all my sins?

But as you look into his eyes, you feel peaceful. There's something about this man. You trust him.

Jesus chooses us because he loves us! His Father is full of mercy, he tells us, and if we repent and believe, we can enter the kingdom of God. We can become like Jesus: loving, kind, and generous. We can join his mission to the whole world.

Are you ready to follow Jesus?

"Jesus, just as you invited Matthew to follow you, you are also inviting me. I renew my yes to you."

March 16

Neither do I condemn you. (John 8:11)

A woman was caught in adultery, a crime punishable by death (see Leviticus 20:10). Jesus' opponents wanted to stone her, but first they asked Jesus what he thought. His one sentence was enough to silence them: "Let the one among you who is without sin be the first to throw a stone at her" (John 8:7).

Why did this one sentence have such a dramatic impact? Because Jesus made it clear that whatever judgment they leveled against this woman for her sin would be leveled against them for their own sins. If she were condemned, they would be condemned too.

Two responses from the Pharisees were possible: to confess their sins or to walk away. Since they were unwilling to repent, they walked away. But the woman stayed, and her life was changed. Jesus showered her with grace and washed away her sins. Even though she was guilty, Jesus issued a decree of divine forgiveness and set her on a new path.

We are moved to change our lives as we experience God's mercy. Like the woman caught in adultery, we deserve punishment but receive love, peace, and life instead.

"Lord Jesus Christ, Son of the living God, have mercy on my soul."

March 17

Teacher, we wish to see a sign. (Matthew 12:38)

The Pharisees saw Jesus heal the sick, cast out demons, and raise the dead. Would another sign really make a difference for them?

What signs has Jesus left us to strengthen our faith? There are historical accounts from the Romans Tacitus and Suetonius and from the Jewish historian Josephus. There is also the New Testament. Nearly six thousand copies of the Greek New Testament and ten thousand copies of its Latin translation exist—and they date back as far as AD 130.

Then there were the apostles. If Jesus weren't God and if he hadn't risen from the dead, there would be no reason for his disciples to dedicate their lives to spreading the good news of the resurrection and to become martyrs for the cause.

That's a lot of signs. The questions left for us are:

"Can I believe that Jesus is who the Scriptures say he is?"

"Can I stake my life on him and his promises?" "What miracles have I witnessed that have pointed to Jesus?"

Let's believe Jesus and give him our hearts today.

"Lord, I believe!"

March 18

*When the people . . . heard this,
they were all filled with fury. (Luke 4:28)*

Jesus was well received by many people in his hometown, but over time, some turned against him. They loved what he said about freeing the oppressed; they weren't so keen on his call to repentance. What did he mean by implying that they needed to be like Naaman or the widow of Zarephath, who weren't even Jews?

Perhaps our response to Jesus is similar. We're swept off our feet when we experience his mercy, but we resist when the Holy Spirit shows us areas of our lives that aren't under his control. Becoming like Christ means humbling ourselves and letting the Lord smooth out our rough edges.

The best way to stay on the path of conversion is to remember why Jesus came—to "let the oppressed go free" (Luke 4:18). God wants us to be free to be united with him and to know his joy and peace. Getting to that place isn't always pleasant, but it's worth it. Seek him, hear his word, and let yourself fall more deeply in love with Jesus!

"Lord, I come to do your will. Fill me with your Spirit so that I can follow you with joy, whatever the cost."

March 19

O woman, great is your faith! (Matthew 15:28)

Jesus healed the Canaanite woman's daughter and commended her faith. Jesus praised the faith of other "outsiders." Consider the centurion who told Jesus, "Lord, I am not worthy to have you enter under my roof; only say the word and my servant will be healed." Jesus responded, "Amen, I say to you, in no one in Israel have I found such faith" (Matthew 8:8, 10).

In singling out people like these, Jesus did more than heal desperate souls. He also showed that faith and trust are the keys to experiencing his power. More than anything else, this disposition makes the difference.

Jesus welcomes anyone who comes to him with an open, humble, and willing heart. If unbelievers can find mercy, surely we can! Jesus doesn't discriminate. His arms are open wide, eager to embrace all of us.

May we take our cue from this woman of faith— an unnamed, humble, and persistent Gentile—and find hope and inspiration in following Jesus.

"Jesus, I am so undeserving of your mercy, but I ask in faith. Just say the word, and I will be healed."

March 20

. . . keeping our eyes fixed on Jesus. (Hebrews 12:2)

Fixing our eyes on Jesus can be a physical action. We look at a cross hanging in our church or in our home, and the image fills us with wonder. On a deeper level, we can fix the eyes of our heart on Jesus and come in touch with the mind of Christ. There we see his tender love for us.

Jesus knows us intimately. He calls to us, "Come to me, . . . and I will give you rest" (Matthew 11:28). As we fix our eyes on him, we know that we can count on him, for "the word of the Lord remains forever" (1 Peter 1:25), "he is always able to save" (Hebrews 7:25), "with age-old love I have loved you" (Jeremiah 31:3), "with [God] there is no alteration" (James 1:17), "I, the LORD, do not change" (Malachi 3:6).

Fix your eyes on Jesus, and let the presence of God become your strength. You will find your time with Jesus becoming the most important part of your day. There you will be lifted up to heaven!

"Lord, I fix my eyes on you. You are the author and perfecter of my faith."

March 21

When someone strikes you on [your] right cheek, turn the other one to him as well. (Matthew 5:39)

Jesus went beyond the Old Testament limit on revenge, "eye for eye, tooth for tooth" (Leviticus 24:20), to get to the heart of the Law: the disproportionate, undeserved mercy of God. Looking at his words through the lens of his death and resurrection, we can see how perfectly he fulfilled this command. But it wasn't only during his final days that Jesus turned the other cheek.

Jesus turned the other cheek every time he endured his opponents' attempts to trap him in his teaching. And again when his own townsfolk tried to kill him and he walked peacefully away. Yet most powerfully, Jesus taught this when he prayed, "Father, forgive them," as he hung on the cross (Luke 23:34). Jesus knows how hard it is to turn the other cheek.

If you should fall to the temptation to seek revenge or to withhold forgiveness, Jesus calls you to do what he has always done: turn the other cheek, forgive, and receive more of his grace.

"Jesus, thank you for your constant mercy and grace!"

March 22

What great nation is there that has gods so close to it as the LORD, *our God, is to us? (Deuteronomy 4:7)*

Moses reminded the Israelites that even though the Law blessed them with God's wisdom, what really set them apart was how close God was to them. In Jesus, God has come even closer.

Jesus revealed the heart of the Law and perfectly fulfilled it. He kept the Sabbath holy not by scrupulously avoiding work but by praying and extending the healing compassion of God to the needy. He did not strike back at those who abused him but forgave them. He kept silent against accusations. He poured his life out in love even for those who condemned him.

Jesus told his disciples, "I have come not to abolish but to fulfill" (Matthew 5:17). He shows us that the heart of the Law is loving God and our neighbor. He shows us that true obedience goes beyond a matter of "thou shalt not." He comes close to each of us to show us what that obedience looks like.

"Jesus, thank you for teaching me how to love."

March 23

Take courage; get up, he is calling you. (Mark 10:49)

The hour has come: Jesus, the great high priest, walks to the place of his Passover sacrifice. On the road to Jerusalem, he issues a call to the blind Bartimaeus. It is a call filled with hope. Bartimaeus throws off his cloak and eagerly approaches Jesus.

What an image! Let us be like Bartimaeus and throw aside everything that limits our expectations. God has marvelous plans for us. Let us allow him to heal our hearts and fill them with the fire of his love. Let us follow Jesus, as Bartimaeus did on receiving his sight.

As adopted sons and daughters of God, we have a royal heritage. Let us persist in calling out to Jesus, as Bartimaeus did, with faith and trust. Let us believe that he will "have pity" on us. He will remove what needs to be removed, strengthen what needs to be strengthened, and give us the grace to get up and follow.

Remember, Jesus is calling you! Can you throw off your cloak, leave your baggage, and follow him?

"Jesus, Son of David, have pity on me! I want to see!"

March 24

We believe that you came from God. (John 16:30)

On the eve of his death, Jesus exhorted his disciples to "take courage" (John 16:33). He was about to face gruesome trials, and yet he offered comfort to his friends.

Jesus knew that the Father was with him, and this "knowing" went beyond logical assent. It was rooted in a deep, personal connection with the Father. Because of that connection, Jesus would hold fast throughout his suffering.

You are created for that same "knowing" that Jesus had. You are fearfully, wonderfully, and exactly made, so that you can know God's presence in you. You can know it because Jesus died and rose, ascended to the Father, and sent his Holy Spirit to live in your heart.

Tell Jesus that you want his truth to take root in you. When situations shake your confidence or threaten your peace, turn to the Lord and ask, "What do you want to tell me here?" His answer may surprise you.

"Jesus, take me into a deeper relationship with you. I want to know you better today than yesterday."

March 25

Come down from the cross now, and we will believe.
(Matthew 27:42)

God didn't release Jesus from the cross—and neither did Jesus try to release himself. By remaining bound to that cross, Jesus broke the chains of sin and death and unbound all of us!

Throughout his earthly life, Jesus exercised a ministry of unbinding. He cast out demons, released people from physical illnesses, and set people free from guilt. He often unbound people on more than one level, healing them physically and liberating them from sin.

Perhaps there are places in our hearts that still need to be unbound. God asks only that we open our hearts and allow him to loosen whatever bond holds us. It may be a habit that has become an addiction. It may be guilt over an unforgiven sin or resentment against someone. It may be a distorted view of who God is and how he looks at us. Whatever it is, we can bring it before the Lord and ask him to unbind us.

"Jesus, I long to experience deeper freedom as a child of God. Come and set me free!"

March 26

Jesus cried out again in a loud voice,
and gave up his spirit. (Matthew 27:50)

Picture yourself with Jesus as he is arrested. Listen to the false charges leveled against him. See him being humiliated by the soldiers. They spit upon him, mock him, and beat him. Jesus remains resolute and focused on his mission.

Now picture him at Calvary. He is exhausted, his body wracked with pain. Nails pierce his hands and feet. The crowd continues to hurl accusations against him. Nonetheless, Jesus looks at you with compassion, understanding, and mercy. He wants your salvation.

Hear Jesus speak to one of the thieves crucified with him. Even now he is leading people to his Father! Finally, hear his loud cry as he hands over his spirit—for you.

Contemplate the events that encompass Jesus' passion. Let them move you to treasure Jesus above all. This is the greatest story ever told.

"Jesus, I am overwhelmed by the love you poured out for me in your passion and death. Thank you, Lord."

March 27

We have been consecrated through the offering of the body of Jesus Christ once for all. (Hebrews 10:10)

On the cross, Jesus gave us everything we need. We grow in faith as we embrace that offering, leading to an ever-deepening realization of all that Jesus has won for us.

Every prayer time is an opportunity to ask Jesus to open our eyes to his love and his wisdom. We can ask him to help us realize his mysteries more fully. And loving Savior that he is, he will give that wisdom.

Consecration to Jesus extends past our prayer time. It moves us to follow him throughout the day, trying our best to stay close to him in good times and in bad.

How can we be consecrated to Jesus today? By looking at the cross and saying, "Thank you, Jesus." By asking Jesus for the faith to help us enjoy life's blessings and respond graciously to its demands. By telling Jesus throughout the day, "I trust in you."

"Jesus, help me put my faith in you every day."

March 28

*God, according to his promise, has brought
to Israel a savior, Jesus. (Acts 13:23)*

Paul is showing the big picture. God's plan has unfolded and now culminates in the sending of the Savior. Everything God promised is true in Christ.

What does God promise us? That if we believe in his Son, we will have eternal life (see John 5:24); that all things will work for our good (see Romans 8:28); and that Jesus will be with us forever (see Matthew 28:20).

God keeps his promises in Christ. No matter what the circumstances of your life may be, keep God's love and his purposes in the forefront of your mind. He loves you, he forgives you, and he invites you to spend eternity with him.

Let this vision inspire you as you rise in the morning and when you go to sleep at night. Let it remain with you throughout the day. Everything else in your life fits into this plan—a plan not just for today and tomorrow but for all eternity!

"Father, thank you for fulfilling your promises. Help me see every aspect of my life as part of your plan for me."

March 29

*In this is love: not that we have loved God,
but that he loved us. (1 John 4:10)*

A machine needs a constant energy source to keep running. Our spiritual engines are no different. We can't love without being filled with God's love. We can't share his compassion and mercy unless we receive them from him. God is the source of our goodness and kindness.

How can we maintain our connection to Jesus? We can pray every day, study Scripture, have good relationships with other believers, and do good works. Above all else, we need Jesus.

The good news is that Jesus loves to meet our needs! He lavishes us with grace as we hear his word. He pours out his power and guidance as we join others in worship. *Jesus' own life within us* makes our lives shine.

When you find it difficult to answer God's call to love, remember to refuel. Jesus is always there for you. He's always ready to embrace you, to feed you, and to build you up.

"Thank you, Lord, for loving me first! Thank you for being my life, my strength, and my joy."

March 30

The Advocate, the holy Spirit that the Father will send in my name—he will teach you everything. (John 14:26)

The Holy Spirit—God living inside of us—is the best teacher in the world, as is his curriculum! The Spirit teaches us about Jesus. His goal is to impart new knowledge and to help us apply that knowledge to our lives.

When we feel overwhelmed, frustrated, or burdened with guilt, the Spirit reminds us of how much Jesus loves us. When we experience a season of blessing and peace, he moves us to thank the Lord.

The Spirit speaks to us all the time, teaching us how to see the world through the eyes of Christ and challenging us in our walk of faith. He nudges us to be kinder, to compliment rather than criticize. He reminds us to serve one another and bless everyone, even people who rub us the wrong way.

Ask the Holy Spirit to teach you today. He will lead you in the way of peace, hope, and encouragement.

"Thank you, Holy Spirit, for opening my mind and my heart. Come and teach me about Jesus today."

March 31

Choose life! (Deuteronomy 30:19)

More than three thousand years after Moses issued this call, God extends the offer to us. He urges us to live according to his ways, so that we can know him and his peace.

We all know this is what God wants, but we also know it's not always easy to make that choice. Our faith may be weak. We may doubt that we can trust Jesus. We may have turned from his path and not be sure how to get back on track.

When we struggle to embrace God's ways, it can be because we have lost sight of who Jesus is and the example he set for us to follow. This is Jesus: the Lord of heaven and earth!

Choose the way of the Lord in the small decisions that you face as well as the big ones. You may experience humbling failures at times. But you can be sure that every time you make the effort, the Holy Spirit unleashes abundant grace to help you and strengthen you.

"Jesus, I choose to follow you. Help me be faithful to this choice in all that I do."

Notes

THE VICTORY
OF THE CROSS

April 1

*Pilate . . . had an inscription written and put on the cross.
It read, "Jesus the Nazorean, the King of the Jews."*
(John 19:19)

If you were to imagine a king in his moment of greatest victory, you probably wouldn't picture someone on a cross. There would be nothing stately or attractive to draw you to him (see Isaiah 53:2). But the Messiah amazes us.

The heart of the gospel message—and the greatest paradox in history—is that Jesus' death on the cross is his moment of victory. Jesus embraced the cross and transformed it into an instrument of mercy and divine power. As he hung there, bleeding and dying, he defeated Satan and emptied sin of all its power.

God invites us to look at the cross and see the life that flows from Jesus' death, the healing that comes from his wounds, and the triumph that comes from his defeat.

See your King in his moment of triumph. His is a victory that can transform your life!

"Lord Jesus, your cross is glorious: something utterly despised you transformed into the source of freedom and joy."

April 2

*The people grumbled against Moses, saying,
"What are we to drink?" (Exodus 15:24)*

The Israelites' journey to the Promised Land was difficult—
and not just because of the harshness of the desert. The
people needed to put aside their grumblings, work together,
and obey God's commandments. The journey called for full
cooperation with God.

We too face trials that call for deep trust and cooperation
with the Lord. Do we lose hope, get impatient, maybe even
grumble and complain?

Or do we look to the cross and stand firm on our faith in
the goodness of the Lord and the victory he has won for us?

No matter what you are facing today, Jesus wants to raise
you up with him and fill you with the joy of his kingdom.
He is the divine healer who wants you to receive the greatest healing of all: faith, so that you can trust in his goodness
and his love for you.

*"Jesus, I place my faith in the victory you have won for me
on the cross. Help me keep my eyes focused on you."*

April 3

You certainly will not die! (Genesis 3:4)

Adam and Eve, surrounded by all the beauty of Eden, gave in to the serpent's temptations. What a contrast to Jesus, who in the harsh wilderness stood fast against the tempter's deceits (see Matthew 4).

Jesus faced the same temptations that Adam and Eve did. Adam and Eve ate the forbidden fruit, while Jesus refused Satan's challenge to turn stones into bread. The serpent convinced our first parents that God was not dealing honestly with them, while Jesus trusted God and refused to test his faithfulness. Adam and Eve were swayed by false promises of power and grandeur, while Jesus chose to submit himself to the Father in humility.

Jesus reversed the pattern of sin. He triumphed over the devil. His victory in the wilderness was a foretaste of the complete victory he would win for us on the cross.

Ponder the daily temptations that you face. Jesus stands with you, offering you a share in his victory. He can make you steadfast. He who promised—he who triumphed—is faithful.

"Jesus, strengthen me with your love, so that I can share your victory over sin and death."

April 4

Raise your heads because your redemption is at hand.
(Luke 21:28)

Jesus encourages his disciples not to be afraid when they see turmoil and troubles. Instead they are to stand erect, because such upheaval is a sign that he is returning.

Jesus tells his disciples to focus on the goal, unafraid of danger, because God is with them. His return will be the fulfillment of everything he has promised. This world may pass away, but God's people will live with him forever.

We who believe in Christ can have great hope amid wars, disease, natural disasters, and other chaos. We know that Jesus, our Savior, is our faithful God who will never abandon us. He is our merciful Redeemer, who gave his life for us. He is our risen Lord, who conquered death and will return to set everything right.

So wait in joyful hope for Jesus' return. Lift your head, and fix your eyes on him. He is with us!

"Jesus, help me fix my eyes on heaven."

April 5

You have faith in God; have faith also in me. (John 14:1)

These words might have sounded alright while Jesus and the disciples were celebrating the Last Supper. But can you imagine how the disciples felt the next day, when Jesus was crucified? The One they hoped would be the Messiah died.

Have you ever had excitement and expectations, and suddenly everything changed? Perhaps your hope died. Even as you went on living, a part of you felt isolated and buried.

Death could not hold Christ in the tomb. Now he wants you to know that you can have faith in him. You can trust that he will restore you and bring you new hope.

Picture Jesus in the room with you. See the smile on his face, and listen to his words: "I want you to know my peace. Can you take a small step of faith toward me?" Release to him your disappointment, frustration, self-blame, guilt, discouragement—whatever you may feel. Have faith in him!

"Jesus, I believe that you are merciful and kind. Help me find new life in you."

114

April 6

May I never boast except in the cross of our
Lord Jesus Christ. (Galatians 6:14)

The Greek word for "boast" (*kauchaomai*) can also be understood as "rejoicing in." And that's what Paul meant here. It was by the power of the cross that he became a new creation, set free from the grip of sin and death.

How freeing is this message for us! We don't have to measure up to impossible standards. We don't have to make ourselves "good enough" for God. He has taken our old, fallen lives and crucified them with his Son. And he has filled us with his Holy Spirit, making us vessels of his very own divine life and love.

Think about all that God has done for you through the cross of Jesus. Sin has lost its power. Death has been destroyed. The gates of heaven are open wide. Nothing can separate you from the love of God!

Boast in the cross of Christ. Boast in his kindness and love. Make this a day of great rejoicing.

"Jesus, all praise and glory are yours! You have made me a new creation, and I rejoice in you."

April 7

His dominion is an everlasting dominion
that shall not pass away,
his kingship, one that shall not be destroyed. (Daniel 7:14)

What is God telling us through Daniel's amazing vision of the winds of heaven, the great sea, and four immense beasts? Biblical scholars say the vision is a creative interpretation of Israel's past and present, ending with the promise that God's justice will prevail. Jesus, "one like a son of man," is coming in victory (Daniel 7:13).

At the end of this age, will we confront turbulence, natural disasters, attempts to deceive the faithful? Yes. All of this has gone on since the fall of our first parents and will continue until Jesus comes again. But no matter what the future holds, we know how the story ends: Jesus is victorious!

Daniel's bizarre tale ends with the everlasting dominion of the Ancient One. That's what we have to hold on to in times of turmoil, confusion, and fear. Take heart! Christ is in you, and he is victorious!

"Jesus, I believe that you have authority over all things. Help me keep my eyes on you."

April 8

If it is by the finger of God that [I] drive out demons, then the kingdom of God has come upon you. (Luke 11:20)

Through Christ, the kingdom of God has broken into the world and overthrown the dominion of darkness. Yet everyday life tells us that Satan is still alive and active in the world. How is this possible?

Jesus did triumph over evil, but that victory continues to work itself out as history advances toward his second coming. Every day the devil tries to win people over to his side, but it's a harder sell. That's because believers are now fully armed against his tactics. We have the Holy Spirit living in us. We have the "armor of God" protecting us (Ephesians 6:11). We have everything we need to win the victory with Christ!

When you are tempted by the evil one, picture yourself at Jesus' feet. Be still, and trust in his grace. Jesus can drive out evil with just one finger. Christ is in you, and he has won every victory.

"Jesus, you have conquered all evil. Help me sit at your feet and rest in his presence today."

April 9

Behold, your king! (John 19:14)

Look at Jesus, your king. See him crowned with thorns. See in his eyes the sorrow for your sins and the joy of his victory over them and over death. His Father will raise him—and raise you with him.

Behold your king! He knows your name. He chose you to be his own, even before you were created. He sees every detail of your life, and he loves you.

Hear him announce, "It is finished" (John 19:30). This is a cry of victory. Your king has completed his mission and opened the gates of heaven for you.

The King of Glory, the One who sustains the universe, hangs on a cross. This king came to serve, not to be served. He conquers not with armies but through sacrifice. He delights in showing mercy, not vengeance.

Let the cross show you what Jesus did for you. Behold your king, and let his sacrifice move your heart. Offer him your love, your trust, and your obedience.

"Jesus, my king, thank you for dying for me. I love you."

April 10

The man had been dwelling among the tombs. (Mark 5:3)

When you read "among the tombs," perhaps you think of a memorial, reminding the man of a past that wouldn't go away. The man found a new place at the feet of Jesus, the One who cared enough to ask him, "What is your name?"

We'd never dream of living in a literal graveyard, but many of us dwell on our sins and mistakes of the past. Condemning thoughts can masquerade as conviction. They drain our hope and leave us burdened with guilt. They do not come from the Lord.

Jesus has come into these tombs to set us free! As you pray today, see yourself at his feet, where every twinge of condemnation yields to the truth of his love. There he reminds you that you are clothed with mercy and forgiveness. He invites you to embrace the freedom and dignity that he has declared over your life. You are a child of God!

Like the man in the Gospel, can we find our home at the feet of Jesus?

"You, LORD, are a shield around me; / my glory, you keep my head high." (Psalm 3:4)

April 11

A little while and you will no longer see me. (John 16:16)

The apostles would feel pain when Jesus was taken from them; they would mourn his death. But they would later be eyewitnesses to his resurrection, and their joy would be complete!

As the spiritual descendants of the apostles, we can have the same joy they did. The Lord has promised he will return. But what about the challenges and trials we face right now, and what about the evil in the world? These things can cause us to wonder whether God has abandoned us.

The answer is: he's never left us. Jesus is not only with us; he's within us, by the power of his Holy Spirit. Call on the Spirit for whatever you need: healing, peace, wisdom, joy!

"Cast your care upon the LORD" (Psalm 55:23), for "neither death, nor life, nor angels, nor principalities, nor present things, nor future things, nor powers, nor height, nor depth, nor any other creature will be able to separate us from the love of God in Christ Jesus our Lord" (Romans 8:38-39).

"Lord, may I see your face and hear your words of hope and encouragement!"

April 12

On the first day of the week,
Mary of Magdala came to the tomb. (John 20:1)

More than two thousand years ago, Jesus' resurrection changed everything: sin was defeated; Satan was vanquished; life swallowed death. This is not just history. It's a present reality that changes everything.

How can we even begin to honor God for what he has done for us in raising Jesus from the dead? We can start like Mary Magdalene, seeking Christ's presence in our own lives every day as our first priority. Let us peer into his empty grave, as she did, and see that Jesus is alive! Jesus reigns victorious from the highest heavens, surrounded by the praise of saints and angels.

And now, he is transforming us. He invites us to reflect the graces of heaven—to be his voice, his eyes, his hands, and his feet to our families, neighbors, friends, and even strangers and enemies.

What action can you take up today to accept this invitation? Let's commit ourselves to Jesus and allow our lives to continue the story of his love and grace.

See Jesus enthroned in your heart. And believe.

"Lord Jesus, you are alive!"

April 13

Look at my hands and my feet. (Luke 24:39)

Jesus proved his resurrection to his disciples by showing them his still-wounded hands, feet, and side. Up to that point, they thought they were seeing a ghost. The wounds were evidence that Jesus was truly alive; he overcame death!

This victory was different from what the disciples had expected. Rather than a king's crown, Jesus bore wounds manifesting the price he paid for our salvation.

Jesus invites us to gaze at his wounds and to see in them the proof of his victory. What's more, he wants us to know that he can turn our own wounds into marks of triumph. There is no situation too desperate for him to overcome.

Jesus, the scarred and wounded Messiah, loves you. He will be faithful to you in your every need. If you ever find yourself doubting this, consider his hands and his feet.

"Jesus, thank you for the marks of your victory! Strengthen my faith in your power to heal and restore."

April 14

Christ has been raised from the dead, the firstfruits of those who have fallen asleep. (1 Corinthians 15:20)

The "firstfruits" of a crop are the first portion harvested. That a part of the crop was ripe implied that the rest of the harvest would follow. Since Jesus has been raised as the "firstfruits" and as a sacrifice to God, it follows that all the dead will rise in due time.

In your prayer today, imagine Jesus, the risen Lord, leading a triumphant parade of all the people he has redeemed—the "second fruits," so to speak. Imagine the people who are now risen with him and enjoying the glory of heaven: the sinful woman who anointed Jesus' feet, Zacchaeus the tax collector, and every other sinner who has been redeemed by the Lord.

And this is our destiny!

What's more, the resurrection doesn't begin at our deaths; Jesus is already making us new creations. He has freed us from sin and guilt, darkness and fear. Today we can experience the first fruits of Jesus' victory.

"Thank you, Jesus, for triumphing over death. Thank you for rising from the dead so that we can rise to new life with you."

April 15

I see the heavens opened. (Acts 7:56)

Before his execution, Stephen announced that he saw the glory of the Lord in an open heaven. Surely this was not Stephen's first encounter with the Lord! Luke describes him as "a man filled with faith and the holy Spirit" (Acts 6:5). Stephen had learned to trust God; he had already experienced the heavens "opening" for him.

An open heaven is not reserved for great saints and martyrs. Through Jesus' cross, the barrier between God and his people—between heaven and earth—has been removed. We who believe can "see" Jesus every day as we turn to him in prayer and read Scripture. Heaven opens for us as we feel his love and find the grace to share that love with others.

At the end of the day, take time to reflect on those moments where your eyes were opened and you saw Jesus' love at work through yourself or through others around you.

"Jesus, thank you for wanting to reveal yourself to me. Help me see you more clearly each day. Come, Lord, and make your presence known!"

April 16

Through their transgression salvation has come to the Gentiles. (Romans 11:11)

The Jews' part in God's plan of salvation is awe inspiring. Throughout history God spoke to them and acted through them—Abraham, Moses, Elijah, Joseph, David, and others— leading to the singular occurrence of God becoming man.

At the pinnacle of the long journey toward salvation for all, the Jews seemed to stumble. Many of them failed to recognize the Messiah, and some even pushed the Romans to execute him.

But God's purpose is firm, and his wisdom is astounding. He turned the error of the Jewish leaders on its head and used it to bring his salvation and love to everyone.

We might not always get it right either. Even when we think we are following God's plan—as the Jewish leaders no doubt thought—we make mistakes. But the good news is that God has a way of using all our mistakes and failings for good. He can redeem every situation, as well as every person!

"Lord, thank you for your great plan and your infinite forgiveness. Help me follow your will, and give me a generous spirit to see everyone as you see them."

April 17

The Spirit said to Philip,
"Go and join up with that chariot." (Acts 8:29)

Imagine that the following thought comes to you while you are praying: *Tell a stranger today how much God loves them.* What would be going through your head? *Did that thought come from me or from the Lord?* Or, *What if the person gets upset with me?*

Do you think Philip had thoughts like these when the Spirit told him to chase down the Ethiopian's chariot? It's possible. But somehow he found the courage to take a risk. And the results were spectacular!

How did Philip get so confident about discerning the Spirit's voice and sharing the gospel? The same way we can: by spending time with Jesus and stepping out in faith.

Maybe all you need is a little practice too. Do you know someone who needs to hear about the Lord? Just a simple question will do: "Do you know that God loves you?"

Try to brighten someone's day. You could start that person on a great adventure.

"God, I trust that you will prepare the hearts of your people, and all I need are a few simple words. Help me take steps in boldness to share the good news with others."

April 18

I shall not die but live
and declare the deeds of the LORD. (Psalm 118:17)

Jesus, you are the risen Lord, and all creation sings your praise!

We hear the stones cry out, just as you said they would, "Blessed is the king who comes in the name of the Lord!" Even the stone that sealed your tomb is rolled away and proclaims a wondrous mystery. Instead of being an immovable testament to your death, it has become an indisputable witness to the resurrection.

Loving Savior, because of you, a cruel instrument of death speaks to us of life. By your cross, you have destroyed the enemy and flung open the gates of salvation. Your light shines in our churches, in our homes, in hospital rooms, in the rubble of warfare, and in many dark and dreary places—proclaiming life to anyone who puts their faith in you.

So many transformed lives! So many signs of victory! Each one, in its own way, speaks to us of you. Let us look, listen, and believe, so that we too may be signs of your victory in our world.

"Jesus, you have conquered death! Show me one new step, however small, that I can take today to 'declare the deeds of the LORD' by my life and words."

April 19

They are like angels; and they are the children of God.
(Luke 20:36)

Jesus taught that everyone is destined for a life that will never end. With Jesus we will inherit all things (see 1 Corinthians 3:21-23), and we will "shine like the sun" in the kingdom of God (Matthew 13:43). We will become like the angels, ministers of God's love and fully submitted to his will.

These blessings of resurrected life are wonderful to think about, but what can we look forward to today? Everything! We can experience these blessings even now, if only in part, because Jesus is already risen and seated with his Father in heaven.

If you were given the choice, which would you choose today? Fear, sin, skepticism, and doubt? Or peace, hope, and unity with Jesus? If you spend your days filled with negative, doubting attitudes that make light of your inheritance, you won't experience your privileged status as a child of God.

Today, choose to live as a child of the resurrection!

"Jesus, I place my hope in you. Help me set my eyes on heaven, so that I can experience your blessings even now."

April 20

Christ did not enter into a sanctuary made by hands.
(Hebrews 9:24)

What is your image of heaven? Will we be with our family and friends? Will we be surprised at who is there—and who is not? What will our glorified body be like? Will we be so caught up in Jesus that we won't be concerned about anything else?

For all our lack of understanding, we can say with confidence that heaven is the fulfillment of our greatest desire: to behold the Lord face-to-face and to live with him forever. Jesus is perfect love, so there could be nothing better.

St. Paul stretches our imagination: "What eye has not seen, and ear has not heard, / and what has not entered the human heart, / what God has prepared for those who love him" (1 Corinthians 2:9). What awaits us is so amazing that words will never be able to describe it.

So keep your eyes on the prize of your heavenly calling. Lift up your head and rejoice, for your redemption is at hand!

"Lord, you have loved me with a love beyond understanding. I worship and adore you, Jesus, for your incomparable gift of salvation."

April 21

Strengthen hands that are feeble,
make firm knees that are weak. (Isaiah 35:3)

Jerusalem was threatened by foreign invasion, and it felt to some that God had abandoned his people. Isaiah countered, "Hold on to your faith!" A time will come when "the parched land will exult; . . . the burning sands will become pools" (Isaiah 35:1, 7).

We all know what it is like to experience dryness in prayer, when we feel no consolation as we try to connect with the Spirit. These are times when we need Isaiah's advice: "Don't give up!"

Times of dryness are opportunities to build our prayer life on the solid truths of our faith.

One good strategy for building our prayer this way is to spend time reading Scripture. We can consider how he has fulfilled his promises and believe that he is still at work.

Place your faith in Jesus' resurrection and continue pursuing God in prayer. Strengthen your weak knees. He rewards those who persist in pursuing him!

"Jesus, thank you for showing me your love. Make me strong in your Spirit, and help me trust in your wisdom."

April 22

We are not discouraged. (2 Corinthians 4:16)

During the course of Paul's ministry, he was beaten, shipwrecked, betrayed, slandered, and imprisoned. Paul was a tough guy by nature, but surely he was not impervious to the stress and strain of the life he had chosen. The key is that he didn't let discouragement overtake him and rule his life.

At the Last Supper, Jesus told his disciples, "Do not let your hearts be troubled. You have faith in God; have faith also in me" (John 14:1). And later, "In the world you will have trouble, but take courage, I have conquered the world" (John 16:33).

These comforting words convey a vital strategy: Hold on to your faith! Trust that the Father and Jesus won't abandon you.

St. Paul assures us that nothing "will be able to separate us from the love of God in Christ Jesus" (Romans 8:39). The knowledge of this truth kept him from giving in to discouragement.

The next time you feel discouragement creeping into your life, think like Paul. Remind yourself that God knows the situation. He is with you. And nothing can separate you from his love.

"Jesus, help me hold fast to your promises."

April 23

Solomon sat on the throne of David his father, and his kingship was established. (1 Kings 2:12)

As King David approached death, he handed over the sovereignty to his son Solomon. Solomon's rule would bring Israel a season of peace and protection, so long as he kept "the mandate of the LORD" (1 Kings 2:3).

Although human rulers often establish their authority through intrigue and power plays, God *invites* us to come under his rule. Jesus, the Lord of all creation, becomes the Lord of our hearts only as we allow him to guide our thoughts and actions—as we welcome him on the "throne" of our lives.

Imagine a throne surrounded by the many aspects of your life: your family, your job, your possessions, your free time, your hopes and dreams. Where is Jesus in this picture? Is he vying with your possessions for a crack at the throne? Or with your job or favorite hobby?

Jesus wants to sit on the throne of your life and rule you with his tender mercy. Open your heart to him!

"Jesus, sit on the throne of my life! Help me trust you more each day."

April 24

God so loved the world. (John 3:16)

Hearts, roses, diamonds. None of these symbols come close to the truest expression of love the world has ever known: the cross of Jesus Christ. God didn't just die for humanity in general; he died for you!

Jesus would have submitted to the pain of the cross even if you were the only person on earth.

How do we respond to so great a love? By opening our hearts and receiving what Jesus died to give us: God's grace and mercy. It is freely poured out on us. Jesus won it at great cost to himself, "becoming obedient to death, / even death on a cross" (Philippians 2:8).

Rejoice! Rejoice that death is upended on Mount Calvary. Rejoice in the blood that destroys strongholds of sin and forges new paths of hope. Rejoice that the kingdom of heaven has become the sturdy foundation of your life.

More than anything else, rejoice because God loves you so much that he sent his Son to save you.

"Jesus, by your holy cross, you have redeemed the world."

April 25

He is our peace, he who made both one and broke down the dividing wall of enmity. (Ephesians 2:14)

St. Paul invited the Ephesians to marvel at the unity they were experiencing. Jews and Gentiles tended to look down on one another, and yet here they were worshipping Jesus together! Through Christ, the centuries-old wall dividing them was broken down, leaving only a bond of love.

About thirty years earlier, "Herod and Pontius Pilate, together with the Gentiles and the peoples of Israel," overcame their differences and put Jesus to death (Acts 4:27). The devil created a false unity in order to eliminate Jesus, but his plan backfired. This mock unity brought about the true unity that Christians everywhere enjoy.

If Jesus can overcome centuries of division between Jews and Gentiles, surely he can heal the divisions in our lives. It may not happen overnight or in the way we expect, but it can happen—especially if we work toward it. So take one relationship today, and offer forgiveness, let go of resentment, or ask for forgiveness, and see what you can do to break down the walls of division. Remember that Jesus is our peace.

"Come, Lord, and heal every division and wounded relationship."

April 26

The days will come when there will not be left a stone upon another stone. (Luke 21:6)

Jesus advises us to look at global catastrophes as "signs of the times." We should not ignore the reality of disturbing events, but none of these are what the end is going to look like.

The end is really a beginning; it is when Jesus returns in glory! Yes, catastrophic events may take place before that day, but these are necessary "labor pains" (Matthew 24:8) because the world isn't ready for Jesus' return.

The Lord will keep us in perfect peace if we put our trust in him (see Isaiah 26:3). How do we do that?

Remind yourself of God's promises. You don't have to fear "the terror of the night / nor the arrow that flies by day" (Psalm 91:5). You can call out to the Lord, "My rock, my fortress, my deliverer" (2 Samuel 22:2). "He will never fail you or forsake you" (Deuteronomy 31:6).

Your mind is where the battle rages. Take your thoughts captive, and rest in God!

"Lord, you are my refuge. Only in you can I find perfect peace!"

April 27

Light dawns for the just,
and gladness for the honest of heart. (Psalm 97:11)

The psalms are full of promises of reward for the just. So why do we sometimes see suffering come to the saintly? Why doesn't the Lord "secure justice for the oppressed" (Psalm 146:7)?

The light that dawns for everyone—the sun—shows us only physical reality. We see by a different light: Jesus, the eternal Son. This light shines on the sufferings of this world and reveals a deeper reality: God is King of all creation, and he offers eternal life to his people.

Christians who are persecuted have found their faith to be a source of strength. This power that brings freedom to the imprisoned and happiness to the oppressed is alive and active today!

We should never lose sight of our hope in the Lord. As we pray for everyone undergoing persecution and for ourselves when we suffer for our faith, let us remember Christ's light on his people. It reveals these situations as opportunities for his victory to be manifest.

"Father, help us live in the light of Jesus Christ, our victor and king!"

April 28

You will see heaven opened. (John 1:51, NRSV)

Some have speculated that Nathanael may have been meditating on God's promises to Israel when Jesus saw him under the fig tree. The prophets and psalms pointed to a peaceful future when God would live among his people and make them a light to the rest of the world. Perhaps reflecting on the glory to come gave Nathanael eyes to recognize Jesus as the Son of God and King of Israel.

Jesus said to Nathanael, "You will see greater things . . . You will see heaven opened" (John 1:50, 51, NRSV). That's what Jesus tells us too. Baptized into Christ, we have been born of water and the Spirit; we have become children of God and citizens of heaven.

Like Nathanael, we can contemplate what heaven will be like. We can picture Jesus surrounded by the angels and saints. We can think about our loved ones there who are praying for us, cheering us on, and rejoicing every time we act in faith.

Sit under your "fig tree" today, lift your heart to the Lord, and let his promises fill your mind.

"Jesus, you have thrown heaven wide open. Lord, let me see your glory!"

April 29

Jesus Christ is Lord. (Philippians 2:11)

When we were dead in sin and Satan was leading the world astray, Jesus Christ accepted death on a cross. Then he rose victorious, freeing us from the power of sin and Satan and making us alive in him.

Jesus triumphed by the cross, and all heaven rejoiced: "God greatly exalted him / and bestowed on him the name / that is above every name" (Philippians 2:9). Let us rejoice and celebrate this victory, with cheering and praises and honor to our God!

Do you see yourself as a conquering hero? You are part of the divine army, and Jesus is your leader. So rejoice in his victory. When pressures and temptations threaten to cloud your heart, stand up, raise your arms, and proclaim, "I am a new creation! Sin has been defeated!" Cling to Jesus, and you can show the world what a triumphant believer looks like.

"Jesus, you freed us from all our enemies and secured our place in heaven. I love you, Lord, and with all creation, I praise the victory of your saving cross."

April 30

Remain in me, as I remain in you. (John 15:4)

Jesus tells us to remain in him. But how do we do that, especially when each day we face a mountain of responsibilities that often take our thoughts away from God? By leaning into him continually—in love, in trust, and in friendship.

This requires a decision on our part to try to reach out to the Lord throughout the day. It can begin in the morning by dedicating the day to him.

You can seek encounters with God as you go about your day. As you are folding laundry, you can sing a song of praise. At the office, you can take a moment to offer him a prayer of gratitude.

As the day progresses, you may feel anxiety welling up in you or experience a moment of sadness or find yourself struggling with temptation. Those are especially important times when you can cry out to God and tell him what's on your heart and then spend a moment listening to see if he has something to say to you.

Who knows? If you try it today, you may become inspired.

"Jesus, you are the vine, I am the branch. May I always be united with you."

GOD PROVIDES
FOR ME

May 1

I will . . . make a house for you. (2 Samuel 7:11)

Rather than allowing King David to build a temple to the Lord, God promises to "make a house" for David! He reminds David that he is the One who has chosen him to become king, destroyed all of Israel's enemies, and brought the kingdom into an era of peace and plenty.

And so God provides for us. He gave us the gift of life. He offers us salvation through his Son. Wherever we go, whatever we do, our generous God is with us.

Imagine: the God of the entire universe has taken a special concern for you, down to every hair on your head (see Matthew 10:30).

Reflect today on God's generosity to you over the past week. Did you sense his presence in prayer? Did he encourage you through the smile of a friend? Did he calm your fears with a sense of his presence? These are all ways he is building a home for you.

"Thank you, Father, for your generosity."

May 2

I trust in you, LORD. (Psalm 31:15)

The world offers many ways to help us handle our health, safety, job security, finances, children. It tells us to work harder, get more training, buy better insurance, or figure out how to influence people. Such responses place our efforts and our fears at the forefront of our minds.

Jesus shows us a different path—the path of humility, surrender, and trust. It's the path of self-giving, not of self-protection. He calls us to follow his way of sacrificial love and to trust that he will care for our needs.

As we reorder our lives to reflect the values of God's kingdom, our cares and worries lose their all-encompassing nature. We become more confident that God will care for us.

So what's worrying you today? Pray Psalm 31, and hand your destiny, your safety, and your family over to the Lord. If you're having trouble letting go, focus on God's love for you instead of whatever is causing anxiety. Ask him how you can imitate his love more fully, and let him take care of everything else.

"Lord, I trust you. Teach me how to live in your love."

May 3

The spirit of the LORD shall rest upon him:
a spirit of wisdom and of understanding,
A spirit of counsel and of strength,
a spirit of knowledge and of fear of the LORD. (Isaiah 11:2)

The gifts of the Holy Spirit are practical tools to help you live a holy, victorious life. God places them in your spiritual tool belt, expecting you to take them out and learn how to use them.

Far from being just concepts, the gifts of the Holy Spirit are very practical in your everyday life. Ask the Holy Spirit to show you what gifts you can use today: perhaps the tool of understanding in relating to a child or wisdom in a work situation.

As you exercise a spiritual gift, God will come alongside and help you. He will give you strength to turn from temptation. He will bring to your mind a "word of wisdom" for a friend who is anxious and doesn't know what to do next.

The more you use spiritual gifts, the more you'll find their giver working with you.

"Thank you, Holy Spirit, for the gifts you have given me.
Help me use them to build your kingdom."

May 4

And I tell you, ask and you will receive. (Luke 11:9)

Have you ever doubted that God has really forgiven your sins? Or that he will fulfill his plans for you? Have you doubted his willingness to bless you?

Jesus challenged his disciples—and each of us—to put aside any doubts about the Father's care. We can almost hear the urgency in Jesus' words: "Seek and you will find. Please, I beg you, knock! Ask my Dad, and you will receive!"

How will you respond to Jesus' directive? The next time you need something, ask God with expectant faith.

We know that he hears our prayers and that he wants the best for us. We've been sealed with the blood of Jesus, so we can approach his throne with confidence. And nothing is impossible for God!

"Lord, thank you for revealing your Father to me! Help me know him as my Father too and to trust in his love and compassion."

May 5

God put Abraham to the test. (Genesis 22:1)

God gave Abraham many opportunities to deepen his faith. And Abraham passed every test with flying colors.

God chose not to tell Abraham exactly where to go but rather pointed him "to the land of Moriah," to "one of the heights that I will point out to you" (Genesis 22:2). The bigger test: would Abraham remain steadfast while heading toward his son's death?

We see why Abraham is called our father in faith (see Romans 4:16). He's an example for anyone trying to follow God.

Certain aspects of our devotion to God might seem absurd to others: getting up early on a Sunday to go to church, letting Scripture guide us on sexual morality, teaching our children virtues that go against prevailing philosophies, giving up our freedom to care for an ailing parent. These actions put our faith in God on display.

Let us take heart. Just as God looked kindly on Abraham's faith, he sees and honors our sacrifices. And as he led Abraham, he will lead us into a closer relationship of trust with him.

"Lord, thank you for seeing my faith. Help me trust you more."

May 6

*To anyone who has, more will be given
and he will grow rich. (Matthew 13:12)*

God designed our bodies in such a way that the more we use them, the better they'll perform. Our faith works in much the same way. Those who "have" receive more.

And what is it that we have? A heart open to the gospel and willing to trust in Jesus.

How you treat the gift of faith is up to you. That truth may scare you a little. If so, try looking at faith as an opportunity and not a risk. To live by faith is to allow God to change you into his likeness. It means planting your little "mustard seed" and letting it grow (Matthew 13:31-32).

Most of us are dealing with at least one challenging situation: a relationship gone sour, a friend who needs healing, a persistent sin problem. These are situations in which Jesus calls us to exercise our faith. We will grow rich, maybe not financially but surely spiritually.

"Lord, help me trust in you more deeply. Give me the courage to exercise my faith."

May 7

Stir into flame the gift of God. (2 Timothy 1:6)

Did you know that fear is a gift from God? It helps us protect ourselves and our loved ones when danger arises. The problem is that our inner gift of fear can become too powerful and cause us to exaggerate the external threats that have given rise to fear.

Most of us become fearful when a significant hardship comes our way. That is a blessing. But we cannot allow these fears to control us. Instead, let's remind ourselves that God is with us, and he is for us. Let's believe that nothing stands against us (see Romans 8:31). And let's never forget that we can do all things in Christ who gives us strength (see Philippians 4:13).

When we place our faith in Scripture passages like these, grace and power are stirred up in us.

"Lord, in your name, I command any spirit of fear to go to the foot of the cross where you died, so that I will not be controlled by it. Jesus, fill me with your spirit of 'power and love and self-control' (2 Timothy 1:7)."

May 8

They picked up the fragments left over—seven baskets full.
(Matthew 15:37)

Jesus is the all-knowing, perfect Son of God. So why didn't he give the apostles exactly the right amount of food for this crowd?

Perhaps Jesus used something as seemingly insignificant as leftovers to teach his disciples something. The number of baskets remaining—seven—can give us a clue.

In Jewish tradition, seven was an expression of the perfection found only in God. It took God six days to create the world, and he rested on the seventh. This Sabbath was a day of satisfaction and plenty, a time to enjoy his creation. Isaiah lists seven gifts of the Spirit (see Isaiah 11:2-3). The Book of Proverbs describes divine wisdom as having seven pillars (see Proverbs 9:1). Jesus told Peter to forgive "seventy-seven times"—that is, always (Matthew 18:22).

Notice that the apostles started with seven loaves and finished with seven baskets. Whenever we rely on God's resources in giving to someone, we will not run out.

What a generous, loving God he is!

"Lord, you alone can satisfy the deepest desires of my heart."

Everything I have is yours. (Luke 15:31)

The older son in Jesus' parable came home to a party in full swing. But he wasn't happy to see his wayward brother so warmly welcomed. He was so caught up in duty, service, and obedience that he missed the most important thing: love, displayed extravagantly and without hesitation.

This is the kind of love that God the Father showers on us every day. It's the kind of love that created the heavens and the earth, the love that set us as rulers over creation. It's the kind of love that sacrificed his only Son for our sake and still forgives and forgives and forgives again. Generous, overflowing, extravagant: the kind of love that boldly declares, "Everything I have is yours." That's how much your heavenly Father loves you.

Your Father delights in you and wants to declare his love for you unmistakably and extravagantly. Listen to that declaration, and be confident in that love.

"Father, I believe that your extravagant love is for me. Help me grow in confidence of your generous provision."

May 10

How much more will your heavenly Father give good things to those who ask him. (Matthew 7:11)

For some people, prayer is sort of like a trip to the casino. Pop in a prayer request, pull the lever, and see what happens. Maybe once in a while they win—a new job, a healing, an unexpected blessing—but more often than not, they're just yanking on the lever and waiting.

Like any father, God wants what is best for us. So we should feel confident that when we don't get what we ask for in prayer, it's because his plan includes a much deeper and more persistent fulfillment than we can imagine.

Of course, we can ask God for anything we think we need, even for things we just plain want. He accepts every prayer we breathe, if only because it's another opportunity for us to come into his presence and for him to shape us. And every time we come to him in prayer, he gently shows us what our hearts really cry out for. We bring him our desires and hopes and dreams, and he transforms them! He helps us learn how to long for things that are truly good for us.

God won't condemn you for being selfish or greedy or misguided. You are precious to him, and he wants nothing more than to make you happy—really and truly happy.

"Father, I trust in you!"

May 11

What do you want me to do for you? (Mark 10:51)

As Jesus leaves Jericho, people crowd around him, each one hoping to bend the Master's ear to their specific needs. Amid that clamor, Jesus hears the voice of Bartimaeus and stops. He listens attentively to the blind man's petition, and then he heals him!

Right now there's an enormous crowd around the globe praying, interceding, and worshipping before the Lord. But no matter how many voices, no matter how loud the entreaties, your voice catches Jesus' ear. He gives you his full, undivided attention and asks, "What do you want me to do for you?"

Jesus shines his light of love upon you right now. Spend time with him. Look to him, and you will discover the graces you need.

Listen to Jesus saying, "Seek me persistently over these next days and weeks. Listen as your friends speak wisdom into your life. Look for my nudges. Watch for me to speak to you through the Scriptures. I will answer you as you yield to me in obedience. Then, in your good conscience, pursue the path, and I will be with you.

"Hear my prayer, Lord. In your faithfulness, answer me."

May 12

The one who had made the promise was trustworthy.
(Hebrews 11:11)

God promised Abraham that he would have "descendants as numerous as the stars" and would become a blessing for "all the families of the earth" (Hebrews 11:12; Genesis 12:3). Abraham believed. Day after day—despite failures and setbacks, despite the twenty-five-year wait for Isaac's birth, despite the fact that he never saw the promises completely fulfilled—Abraham kept believing.

Abraham staked his life on the fact that he had a call from God and that "the one who had made the promise was trustworthy." He shows us how our faith and passion for God grow: personal encounters with the Creator motivate us to put our faith to work.

Have you heard Jesus calling? Do you know what he wants you to do and to be?

Thank the Father for his wonderful purpose in creating you. Tell Jesus that you want to follow him more closely. Ask the Holy Spirit for a holy passion for the rest of the journey.

"Here I am, Lord. Where will you lead me today?"

May 13

Take . . . no food, no sack, no money. (Mark 6:8)

We all have days when we feel empty-handed and unprepared to do the work of the Lord. We might say to ourselves, "God hasn't given me enough patience" or, "I wish I had the same compassion that so-and-so has." In these moments, we can consider the "no food, no sack, no money" principle. What may seem to be an extreme example of packing light was Jesus' way of asking his disciples to trust him.

When we try to follow God on our own strength and wisdom, we will find ourselves unprepared. But when we trust that God will care for us, we'll find him coming through with unexpected grace. He will "give us this day our daily bread."

Ask God to fill you with all the provisions you need for your journey. Let him relieve you of the burden of trying to provide for yourself. Tell the Lord what you think you're missing. Ask for his help. He won't leave you empty-handed.

"Jesus, in my weakness, I rely on your strength. Give me my daily bread, so that I can accomplish your work."

May 14

God . . . gives to all generously. (James 1:5)

James gives us a lot of advice: be joyful when you suffer; persevere; ask in faith; recognize the fact that you will fade like a flower. But he doesn't leave us to work away at all this. He reminds us that God has given us his grace and delights in giving us even more of it.

You have received this grace. How can you tell? As you grow in prayer, you might find yourself more willing to forgive a coworker or friend. You might be more patient with your children than you were last year. You might pray for someone in need rather than feeling powerless. These are signs that God is pouring grace upon grace into your heart. Say a quick prayer of thanks!

Be aware and mindful of these moments. You are seeing the face of God at work in your life.

God never tires of giving us his gifts. You can ask him for wisdom and for help when you find yourself lacking.

Follow the advice of James, but don't try to do it on your own!

"Father, I trust your generosity. I believe that you have poured grace into my life and that you have even more grace waiting for me."

May 15

O woman, great is your faith!
Let it be done for you as you wish. (Matthew 15:28)

The Canaanite woman knew that she had no business going to a Jew with her request. Her desperation overpowered that concern. Jesus was the one man who could heal her daughter.

Jesus in turn commended the woman for her faith. But faith is only one of her virtues. She showed determination as well.

Living in faith is not just a matter of resting peacefully in God's arms, trusting that everything will turn out well. There are times when faith means fighting through obstacles for what God wants to give us, coupling our faith with strength of will.

If you ask the Lord for a job, you will still check job postings and go to interviews. If you ask him to heal a relationship, you can still reach out to that estranged friend. God applauds your efforts to put your faith into action.

Let's be firm in our faith, act on it, and trust in God's provision.

"Jesus, help me take steps in faith, confident that you will carry me the rest of the way."

May 16

Woman, how does your concern affect me?
My hour has not yet come. (John 2:4)

Many stories in Scripture speak of people "changing" God's mind. Abraham negotiated with God over the fate of Sodom (see Genesis 18:16-33). A Canaanite woman asked Jesus three times to heal her daughter, and he finally relented (see Matthew 15:21-28). Jesus told the parable of the persistent widow who changed a judge's mind (see Luke 18:1-8). And though Jesus seemed to deny his mother's request at the wedding feast, he provided wine in abundance!

How can we persuade the one who declares, "As I have resolved, / so shall it be," and, "The LORD of hosts has planned; / who can thwart him?" (Isaiah 14:24, 27).

What a mystery is born when human faith meets the sovereignty of God! God is completely in control, and he bends low to answer our prayers and draw us to work out his plan. We will understand this mystery only when we see Jesus face-to-face. But for now, let us revel in it. How wondrous are the ways of God!

"Lord, you inspire awe in my heart. Who is like you?"

May 17

Cast all your worries upon him because he cares for you.
(1 Peter 5:7)

Your heavenly Father cares about your struggles, your questions, and your efforts to understand how and why he made you. He promises to "restore, confirm, strengthen, and establish you," even if you endure suffering for a while (1 Peter 5:10).

The promise of the gospel is that you can receive from your heavenly Father whatever you need. Any area of your life that you think is uncontrollable—an eating disorder, loneliness, financial worry, trauma—you can tell your Father all about it.

Ask your heavenly Father for wisdom and understanding. Seek from him the courage to face the obstacles that your life presents. Ask him for the strength and perseverance to work through issues. Tell him about the things that seem too heavy for you to carry. Repent if you need to, and move into greater freedom.

Trust God; he really does care for you. He is working in power and wisdom beyond anything you can imagine.

"Father, take my pain, my fear, my sorrow. Fill me with the assurance of your love and care for me."

May 18

Teacher, do you not care that we are perishing?
(Mark 4:38)

It must have wounded Jesus' heart to be rebuked as an uncaring master when all he was doing was waiting for the disciples to call out to him. "Why are you terrified? Do you not yet have faith?" (Mark 4:40). Jesus patiently waits also for us to recognize our limitations and invite him to act.

Perhaps you feel that you have waited too long for an answer to prayer. You might be interceding for people's conversions and wondering why Jesus isn't "zapping" them with his power so that they will believe. It may seem as if Jesus is asleep in the boat, deaf to your cries.

Imagine Jesus standing beside the people for whom you're praying. Picture them as their hearts soften. See their eyes opening wide as they spy Jesus through the wind and rain of their storms. Keep on praying, confident that Jesus never passes by anyone in a storm. He has his own timing, wisdom, and plans.

"Jesus, you know who is on my heart when I cry out to you. Help me be persistent yet patient as you work in their lives."

May 19

Please, come. (Mark 5:23)

Every parent wants the best for his or her children. When children are doing well, fathers rejoice, and mothers give thanks for God's blessings. But children's lives can get messy, cracked, or just plain broken. Every parent knows what it's like to turn to the Lord and plead, "Please, come."

The good news is that God always comes. If you have children, run to Jesus in prayer every day, and lay them at his feet. Ask him for wisdom. Ask him to make you strong and loving, patient and compassionate. Reach out and touch Jesus, and let his power be released in your family.

God is more invested in your children than you are! His love for them is deep, strong, and everlasting.

Imagine how tenderly Jesus took the hand of Jairus' little girl as he raised her from death. He sees you and your family with that same tenderness of heart. You are all in his strong, gentle hands.

"Jesus, I bring my family before you right now. Please come and release your healing love and grace into our lives."

May 20

The LORD is our God, the LORD alone! (Deuteronomy 6:4)

Against a bewildering landscape of deities, the Jews stood in stark contrast in their worship of one God. What's more, he was the only true God, the One behind all the forces of nature.

We too worship the only God, the omnipotent, omniscient, singular God yet a Trinity of divine Persons. He is above all else, subject to no other force. He is more than equal to anything that confronts us.

Money shortages, family troubles, personal shortcomings, lack of faith—whatever your concern, remember that our God has the ultimate power. Nothing is outside his domain. He holds all things together!

The next time you are waylaid by cares, frightened or frustrated or angry, take heart! God is infinitely capable. Not only that, but he is eager to help you. Trust in him, because "the LORD is our God, the LORD alone!"

"Lord, I praise you for your immense power and majesty. Thank you for your love and your dominion over every area of my life."

May 21

I, in turn, give him to the LORD. (1 Samuel 1:28)

Samuel was clearly a gift from God. Hannah, a once barren woman, recognized her son as a sign of God's favor. This generosity of God moved her to be generous in return.

When we receive a gift, we can say thank you and maybe give a gift in return. Hannah shows us that we can also consecrate a gift to God—that is, use it in a way that serves and glorifies him.

Are we grateful for all that God has done for us and all that he has given us?

Does his love moves us to love him in return?

God wants to give you tangible evidence of his love. He loves you; he always has, and he always will. Take this truth with you throughout the day, and let it move you to imitate Samuel's mother by consecrating your gifts and talents to the Lord.

"Father, with a grateful heart, I consecrate everything you have given me. May these gifts bring you glory and turn others' hearts toward you."

May 22

Today the LORD shall deliver you into my hand.
(1 Samuel 17:46)

Wouldn't it be wonderful to throw a rock at your problems and watch them disappear? There is more to this story than David's bravery. He relied on the Lord to give him victory.

God wants us to learn the combination of faith and action that David showed. Do we rely too much on God and neglect the work that he calls us to do? Or do we rely on our own strength, doing the "work of the Lord" but neglecting the "Lord of the work"?

The first approach can leave us fruitless and frustrated; the second, full of ourselves or worn out. Cooperation between divine grace and human work brings fruitfulness, refreshment, and joy.

We are weak without the Lord, but we can do all things through Christ who strengthens us (see Philippians 4:13). Let us be still and know that he is God (see Psalm 46:11), then step out and do our part.

What Goliath are you facing? Trust in God's power as you fling your stone.

"Jesus, I place my confidence in your power and in the talents you have given me."

May 23

The fervent prayer of a righteous person is very powerful.
(James 5:16)

Prayer is a loving conversation between you and God. It may seem like a gentle, quiet activity, but it has the power to change things dramatically. As you sit with the Lord in prayer, he brings healing to your spirit, mind, and body. Prayer turns weakness into strength and fear into confidence. It brings comfort when you mourn and understanding in places where you have known only disagreement.

Prayer will change your heart. It helps you repent and forgive. It brings freedom from sin, Satan, and worldly influences.

Prayer accomplishes things in the people around you. When you know firsthand what God can do because he has done it in you, your prayer for other people naturally increases in intensity and in power. You can give other people what you have received: God's love, his healing, his wisdom, his mighty power.

"Father, help me experience your power at work in me today as I pray. Heal me, change me, and fill me with your love."

May 24

One's life does not consist of possessions. (Luke 12:15)

Jesus told a parable in which he called a rich man a fool because of where he placed his hope. "Bigger storehouses! That's the ticket," the rich man reasoned when he had an exceedingly good harvest. With storehouses full of food and goods, he was sure he would live a worry-free life.

Imagine if the man had placed the Lord of the harvest ahead of the harvest itself. Then the source of his hope would not have been one prosperous season but the One who is the provider and sustainer of life.

Here's one way to look at it. Once you turn on your television, it stays on only because it continues to draw power from an electrical source. When you turn it off, it no longer has "life." In a sense, we are similar. We have life because God is sourcing our lives, and we will enjoy that life only to the degree that we are "plugged into" it.

As we maintain continuous contact with the Lord, we will thrive. We will experience his joy and freedom, power over temptation, peace amid life's challenges, and a lasting sense of dignity and purpose.

"Lord, I choose to hope in you rather than in earthly wealth. Riches may come and go, but you are unchanging. You are my true treasure."

May 25

You are being enriched in every way for all generosity.
(2 Corinthians 9:11)

In other words, God is blessing you abundantly so that you can bless other people.

Paul was talking about material blessings and about spiritual ones as well. As he told the church in Ephesus, God has "blessed us in Christ with every spiritual blessing" (Ephesians 1:3). God sent his only Son so that we would know his love and mercy. This richness in Christ can move us to generosity.

Consider all the ways God has provided for you, and ask him how you can share them. Perhaps he will inspire you to give to the poor. Perhaps you can donate time to your church or a charity. Maybe God has blessed you with a rich prayer life, and you can intercede for other people's needs.

God is a cheerful giver. Cheerfully he gave us his Son, forgives our sins, showers us with mercy, and pours his love into our hearts. Let's ask him for the grace to be as cheerful a giver as he is!

"Father, thank you for all you've given me. Show me how to share it."

May 26

I will put enmity between you and the woman,
and between your offspring and hers;
he will strike your head,
and you will strike his heel. (Genesis 3:15, NRSV)

Adam and Eve didn't trust that God would provide them with everything they needed. God's response shows how wrong Adam and Eve were. Although he cast them out of Eden for their disobedience, he kept providing for them: fruit from the earth, clothing of animal skins, children, and more.

Far from washing his hands of the human race, God promised to save us. He sent us Jesus, who took all our sins on himself and forgave the offense that cast us out of paradise. And because of Jesus' act of supreme goodness, we can come to the Father, who fills us with every good and perfect gift.

Don't miss out on the gifts God offers you. Place your trust in your heavenly Father. You can experience the awesome reality of a loving God who showers you with grace. He is always faithful, and his mercies are always new.

"Dear Lord, thank you for sending your Son so that I can have life and have it abundantly."

May 27

*Stand your ground and see the victory the
LORD will win for you today. (Exodus 14:13)*

The Israelites left Egypt overflowing with riches, freed
from slavery, and having witnessed ten awe-inspiring
plagues. Yet their immediate response to the approach of
Pharaoh's army is "Were there no burial places in Egypt that
you brought us to die in the wilderness?" (Exodus 14:11).

When a crisis rears its head, how easy it is to lose our
peace and trust. Fortunately, God proves to us that his love
is strong, steady, and unchanging. And God is patient! He
works with us, that our trust in him may grow.

As we become more confident in God, we'll be set free
from fear. "If God is for us, who can be against us?" (Romans
8:31). We'll find strength to give ourselves to others in love.
No one can snatch us from the Father's hand (see John 10:29).

Take a moment to picture yourself on the shores of the
Red Sea. Imagine whatever threats you are facing, and let
God show you how to "go forward" in the confidence that
he is by your side.

*"Lord, I put my trust in you today. Help me rely on you in
every situation."*

May 28

He does not ration his gift of the Spirit. (John 3:34)

Our heavenly Father's love is inexhaustible. He holds nothing back from us. There is always more available for the asking.

A beautiful prayer recited during the Jewish Passover meal includes the following words: "God, if you had only created us, it would have been enough for us. God, if you had only freed us from slavery in Egypt, it would have been enough for us." The prayer lists many blessings and concludes with the statement: "How much more do we have to be thankful for the manifold and unbounded blessings of the All-Present God!"

What a great prayer for us today! No matter how much we realize all that God has done for us, there is always more.

What does your list of blessings include? Think of the ways your heavenly Father has provided for you and revealed his love to you. Think too of the blessings you hope to see in years to come. Rejoice in his boundless gifts in your life—past, present, and future.

"Lord, if you had only forgiven my sin or removed my guilt, it would have been enough. But you have done so much more. All praise to you!"

May 29

Do you want to be well? (John 5:6)

What is the condition of your spiritual health? While our physical problems can loom large, Jesus is just as concerned with our spiritual illnesses—our attachments to sin and our avoidance of his ways.

When Jesus asked the sick man if he wanted to be well, the man didn't answer directly; he instead complained about his situation. This gives us a clue that this man's problems were more than physical. Maybe he was reluctant to be healed. He was used to living with his sickness, and being well might entail a new kind of life that could be scary. After healing him, Jesus told him not to sin anymore, "so that nothing worse may happen to you" (John 5:14).

Jesus may choose to heal your body, but he definitely wants to heal your soul. He promises great joy as you put your sins aside and follow him.

"Jesus, help me be open to the healing you want to do in my life."

May 30

Enlarge the space for your tent. (Isaiah 54:2)

God's promise to bless his chosen people sheds light on how he wants to bless us today. *Enlarge your tent, he urges us. Change your expectations.*

"The love of God is broader than the measure of our mind." So goes a line from an old hymn. God's plans are bigger than our plans. Look at David, who wanted to build a temple, and God built him a dynasty (see 2 Samuel 7). Peter went out to catch fish, and Jesus made him a fisher of men (see Luke 5:1-11). A Samaritan woman went to a well for water, and Jesus offered her living water (see John 4).

What are your dreams? Give them to the Lord. God's plan may look completely different from what you expect, but it will be exactly what you need. God is with you, so "raise a glad cry" (Isaiah 54:1)!

"Lord, I thank you in advance for your generosity to me!"

May 31

God shall give them light, and they shall reign forever and ever. (Revelation 22:5)

Have you ever thought about what heaven might be like? You might call John's vision in Revelation the happy ending to our story. Imagine what the glorious day of Christ's reign will be like. Let's lift our hearts and praise God for all that he has planned for us!

Thank you, Lord, for offering me refreshment in a "river of life-giving water, sparkling like crystal" (Revelation 22:1). You satisfy my thirst for meaning, love, and joy!

Praise you, Lord, for healing and strength from the "tree of life" (22:2)! You offer me its delicious fruit!

You tell me, "Nothing accursed will be found . . . anymore" (22:3). You will wipe every tear from my eyes and remove all death and mourning, wailing and pain.

Lord, you promise that "night will be no more" (22:5), for you will become my light.

Lord, I will see you face-to-face! I will see you and belong wholly to you!

Thank you, Jesus, that you walk with me and draw me to your side for my own happy ending!

"Jesus, thank you for the promise of heaven. I trust in you."

172

Notes

June

GOD GIVES
HIMSELF TO ME

June 1

Remove your sandals from your feet,
for the place where you stand is holy ground. (Exodus 3:5)

In Egypt, where Moses grew up, people were required to go barefoot before Pharaoh or any other superior as an expression of respect. Standing before the Lord of all, Moses must have felt awed and humble indeed.

Prayer is also a place of "holy ground" because we are standing before the Lord. Without any burning bushes to jolt us, it's easy to come to prayer and relate to God casually, or even as if prayer is something of a chore. But our loving Father is an awesome God whose holiness we cannot begin to comprehend.

How can we approach him with reverence and humility?

Shoes and sandals get dirty, and "grimy footwear" can symbolize the distractions that pop up when we pray. Let's do our best to leave extraneous thoughts at the door of our prayer place. As one holy man would say, "O my thoughts, wait here. After prayer we shall speak about other matters."

So as you go to pray today, take off your sandals! The One who called Moses is calling you!

"Father, help me set aside everything that separates me from you and return your love as fully as I can."

June 2

The skin of his face had become radiant while he spoke with the LORD. (Exodus 34:29)

The light of God radiated from Moses because he had received God's word, not just on tablets of stone but also in his heart.

Has God's word changed you?

Perhaps you do not see evidence of a change, at least nothing so dramatic as Moses' shining face. But when you hold your tongue instead of joining in gossip, your witness shines. When you share stories about your faith with others, you show how God's word has changed you. Simply attending church on Sunday is evidence that the word of the Lord has found a place in your heart.

Your face may not shine as Moses' did when you go out of your way to help a friend or when you offer forgiveness to someone who has wronged you. But God's presence and the warmth of his love radiate to people around you. All because the word of God has found a place in your heart.

"Thank you, Jesus, for your word, which has changed me. Lord, help me reflect your love even more today!"

June 3

Dwell in the shelter of the Most High. (Psalm 91:1)

During his years of ministry, Jesus faced many challenges. Pharisees challenged him. John's disciples wanted clarification. A woman wanted to be healed. A father wanted his daughter back. Mourners ridiculed him.

How did Jesus keep his focus and his peace amid all the chaos?

He rested "in the shelter of the Most High" (Psalm 91:1). He spent time with the Father. He stepped back from the pleas and pressure, put everything aside, and listened. He asked questions, sought wisdom, and made it his business to know his Father's thoughts and desires.

Jesus is your model and your mentor.

As you read Scripture, let God show you his heart. You can ask him questions and expect the Spirit to put answers in your mind and heart. You can sit quietly with him and just listen.

Settle "in the shade of the Almighty" (Psalm 91:1) and let him be your refuge.

"Father, I want to dwell in your shelter today. Refresh me, and help me walk in peace, focused on the business you have for me."

June 4

I will allure her now;
I will lead her into the wilderness
and speak persuasively to her. (Hosea 2:16)

The prophet Hosea spoke to a people who were turning from their covenant relationship with God and embracing pagan religions.

Why would God woo his people rather than upbraid them for their infidelity?

God, our divine spouse, always takes the initiative. He takes steps toward us even when we are unfaithful to him. His purpose in the eighth century BC was not to castigate Israel for their sins but to win their hearts again. He wanted them to know his commitment to them, his faithful love, and his willingness to forgive every sin.

Come away with God to "the wilderness," to a place free of distractions. Let him speak to your heart. Let him convince you of his faithfulness and his love. He is focused on one thing: drawing you and everyone to his side. So turn your heart to him, and let him woo you.

"Lord, help me quiet my heart. I trust that your love is leading me."

June 5

The LORD is God! The LORD is God! (1 Kings 18:39)

The prophets of Baal tried everything to rouse their god, to no avail. Elijah, on the other hand, prayed: "LORD, God of Abraham, Isaac, and Israel, let it be known this day that you are God in Israel and that I am your servant and have done all these things at your command. Answer me, LORD! Answer me, that this people may know that you, LORD, are God and that you have turned their hearts back to you" (1 Kings 18:36-37).

How should we draw near to God?

Elijah gives us three clues to prayer:

First, remember. He reminded the Israelites that their God was the faithful One who sees, hears, and answers his people.

Second, speak simply. He used simple, direct language.

Third, trust God. He believed God would answer his prayer.

Sometimes God answers prayers in ways that are unexpected, even undesired. We must continue to remember who God is, to speak simply, and to trust.

We have God's attention. He loves us and wants to hear all that is on our heart.

"Thank you, Father, for hearing my every prayer. You are my hope."

June 6

Arise and go down to the potter's house;
there you will hear my word. (Jeremiah 18:2)

There was nothing extraordinary about a potter's house. But God decided to enter an ordinary moment and transform it with his word. He promised Jeremiah that, just as the potter made a new dish from a blemished piece of clay, he would mold Judah until they were completely pleasing to him. This is the kind of intimate relationship God wanted with his people.

God is present too in our everyday lives. Whether we are at work, sweeping a floor, or making a meal, he longs to speak to us, to mold our hearts, and to form our minds.

God is unlimited in his ways. He may remind you of a passage from Scripture while you sit in traffic. He may whisper words of love to you in the middle of the night. He may remind you of his patience while you wait in the doctor's office.

Will you welcome God into every part of your day?

Keep your heart open—be molded by the Master Potter!

"Thank you, Father, for being in every part of my life. Speak to my heart, and mold me into your own image."

June 7

He will change our lowly body to conform
with his glorified body. (Philippians 3:21)

Paul must have felt excited as he wrote to the believers in Philippi. They would have also been delighted to consider how God's power would one day complete their transformation into the very image of Jesus Christ.

Envision a heavenly snapshot of the you who will inhabit eternity. Your eyes glimmer with light reflected from the Son of God. You grin widely because you taste the eternal fruit of following the Lord. Every burden is lifted, every inner hurt healed. God's imprint of his personality is uniquely revealed in you.

This person is the you whom even now the Spirit is working to uncover. Through the storms, trials, stretching, and monotonies of life, the old version of you is falling away, and "Christ in you, the hope for glory" (Colossians 1:27) is being revealed.

If you hunger for a spiritual breakthrough, carry it to the Lord in prayer. Ask him to help you. And be on the lookout for evidence of changes taking place.

"Lord, take me! Melt me, mold me, and use me."

June 8

Keep yourselves in the love of God. (Jude 21)

Jude isn't telling us to work hard so that our Father will love us. His words speak rather to the way we use the precious gift of memory. We need to keep alive the memory of God's love for us, so that we can continue to think and act in ways that honor the Lord.

The feelings of joy and happiness we experience when we pray can fade, and difficult times can threaten our peace.

Take some time today to recall past events that prove God's love for you—times of prayer or situations in which you've felt God's hand on you.

This is how you build up your database of trust and faith in him. You can draw upon this database to help you stay rooted in his love.

It is vital that we all keep our memories clear and active so that we can stand on the truths of the Lord. So let us worship him and listen to him every day.

"Jesus, I trust in your mercy and love. Help me remember you every day—you who are my Lord, my Savior, and my friend."

June 9

The kingdom of heaven is like a merchant searching for fine pearls. (Matthew 13:45)

When we read this parable, we usually think of ourselves as the merchant in search of treasure. Another interpretation sees God as the merchant and each of us as the treasure. It tells us how dedicated our heavenly Father is to winning our hearts. He will stop at nothing to possess us as his very own.

God speaks to us in many ways, trying to capture our attention and our imagination. He even sent his Son, who sacrificed his life for us. It was a costly sacrifice indeed, which shows how valuable we are to him.

You are the pearl of great price, God's highest treasure. He has searched far and wide for you and is overjoyed to find you. He sees the beauty and glory inside you and is committed to cleaning and polishing you until you glow with the radiance of his life.

"Praise to you, Father, for your loving pursuit of me! Praise to you, Jesus, for giving all you had in order to make me your own! Praise to you, Holy Spirit, inexhaustible source of cleansing and renewal!"

June 10

A sound started up, as I was prophesying, rattling like thunder. The bones came together, bone joining to bone.
(Ezekiel 37:7)

God seems to enjoy making impossible things a reality. Think of a universe unfolding from nothing; of a crucified man, buried for three days, erupting out of hell, then appearing to his disciples. Could this God be intimidated by any of our prayer requests? Now, that's an impossible idea!

Think about "dry bones" in your life, your seemingly impossible prayers or dreams. Perhaps an end to abortion, a child's return to the Lord, or the mending of a relationship. Before bringing these before the Lord, consider what God asked Ezekiel: "Can these bones come back to life?" (Ezekiel 37:3).

Maybe only God knows. Maybe he has a better plan, something you cannot yet fathom. As you pray, you will come to embrace that plan—a plan that promises new life for all your dry bones, in his time and according to his wisdom.

It takes courage to prophesy over dry bones, but you can be confident. "For God all things are possible" (Matthew 19:26).

"Lord, help me walk through the valley of dry bones and believe."

June 11

But Ahaz answered, "I will not ask!
I will not tempt the LORD!" (Isaiah 7:12)

Do you believe God is interested in the details of your daily life or that he cares enough to manifest himself to you in a personal way? Like King Ahaz, we may resist the idea of asking God for a sign. But a sign can be exactly what we need to move us along the path to spiritual maturity.

We can easily decide between a clear good and a blatant evil. But more often, two good alternatives are placed before us. God trusts us to make a good decision, and he promises to walk with us along either branch of the path. In deciding, we long to know what God thinks, but it may be appropriate to ask God for a sign.

That sign may take many forms. Sometimes the sign is a spoken word that resonates in our heart. Sometimes it's something in nature, like a rose blooming out of season. Sometimes the Spirit leads us to a passage in Scripture that speaks to us.

God isn't a magician. When you sense him leading you, test it. Seek the advice of trusted mentors. Wait until you are at peace that this is God's word to you. Then move forward with confidence, and let God work.

"Father, I delight in doing your will. Make your way clear before me."

June 12

What, then, will this child be? (Luke 1:66)

Even before he was born, John the Baptist leapt for joy in the presence of Mary and Jesus. King David also leapt before the ark of the covenant as he brought it to its place of honor in Jerusalem (see 2 Samuel 6:14-15). The prophet Isaiah wrote that in the age to come, when the glory of the Lord is made manifest, the lame will leap for joy (see 35:4-6).

All this leaping shows us that there is a part of us that can recognize God, regardless of what we do or who we are. It's encoded into the way he made us. The Holy Spirit wants to bring this to life. He wants us to recognize Jesus and rejoice in his presence, even if Jesus comes to us in unlikely, humble ways.

The relationship between John the Baptist and Jesus is something we all can experience. We can leap for joy as we prepare this world for the coming of Christ the King!

So raise your level of awareness, and recognize Jesus' presence in your life today.

"Lord, I want to see you. Come show yourself to me, and fill my heart with joy."

June 13

In praying, do not babble. (Matthew 6:7)

How am I supposed to pray? What should I pray for? What is successful prayer?

Jesus distilled it down to its essential elements: keep it simple; persist; line yourself up with God and his plan.

More words don't always translate to better prayer. In fact, the less we speak, the more time we have to listen to God.

Jesus gave us the Our Father: We worship God ("hallowed be thy name") and submit ourselves to him ("thy will be done"). We trust him to provide for us ("give us this day our daily bread") and realign ourselves with him and other people when we have fallen short ("forgive us . . . as we forgive"). And we ask humbly for his protection ("deliver us from evil").

As we spend time with God, commit ourselves to following his will, and listen closely for his voice in our hearts, he makes us more like him. That's the key to "successful" prayer.

"Jesus, thank you for teaching me to pray with simplicity. Help me follow your example."

June 14

I will let him whose way is steadfast
look upon the salvation of God. (Psalm 50:23)

If you went to a doctor and discovered that you had a dangerous but curable illness, would you ignore your diagnosis and walk out the door?

As illogical as this sounds, this is the approach we often take in our spiritual lives. Our spiritual sickness is sin, Jesus is our doctor, and faith and repentance are our remedy. God promises that he will not only forgive us, but he will also show us salvation. When we sense God putting his finger on an area of sin, we might think, "It's not that big a deal."

But God isn't trying to pound us. Quite the opposite! He pleads with us to remove the sin that blocks us from receiving his love.

Your divine Doctor reaches out to you all the time. He constantly points you toward salvation. So welcome those moments when you feel a sense of godly guilt or conviction of sin. They are special times of grace, when Jesus wants to heal you and set you free.

"Holy Spirit, thank you for the gift of repentance!"

June 15

She was moved with pity for him. (Exodus 2:6)

What might have happened if Pharaoh's daughter hadn't saved the baby Moses from the river? She may seem like a minor character in the story of salvation, but she played a vital role in the deliverance of Israel. And in a sense, she mirrored the God who would deliver the Israelites from slavery in Egypt.

What situations move your heart? It might be the sight of an impoverished child or the realization that many people go hungry and cold every day. It could be the loneliness of a coworker or the exhaustion of a neighbor working two jobs just to make ends meet.

The urge to respond to such situations can get lost amid everything else you have to do. But considering what "moves you with pity" might show you where the Lord wants you to act. You can make a difference in someone's life! You have a chance to be Christ to someone.

What things touch your heart?

Do whatever it takes to respond to the little tugs the Lord puts there. Who knows? You just might help the next Moses!

"Lord, move my heart, and help me act today."

June 16

Does God belong to Jews alone?
Does he not belong to Gentiles, too? (Romans 3:29)

Salvation is meant for all who believe (see Romans 3:22). Every person is a treasure to him—even those who appear to be lost.

This is the wonder of the gospel message. Through Jesus, God has shown extravagant love to the whole world. He has opened the door of salvation to Jews and Gentiles, to the religious and the atheist, to the rich and the poor, to the young and the old. All are on equal footing beneath the merciful cross of Jesus, for "there is no partiality with God" (Romans 2:11).

We have the privilege of helping people experience the knowledge that God wants them to be with him forever. The drivers, walkers, shoppers, and workers we see every day are all special treasures of the Lord. We can enter the picture by praying for them.

Do we see treasure in the people around us? Do we see them as God's children?

Ask the Holy Spirit to open their hearts. Ask the Father to send people who can share the good news with them. Pray that they come to experience the joy of belonging to the Lord. Your prayer can move mountains!

"Lord Jesus, thank you for belonging to everyone."

June 17

He willed to give us birth by the word of truth.
(James 1:18)

Our spiritual birth brings joy to the Father's heart. He wants us to grow in that initial faith, and so we need to keep encountering the word of truth.

Scripture is a sure place to encounter Jesus. We can imagine ourselves accompanying Jesus on his journeys, or we can picture him teaching us. As we do this, Jesus strengthens our faith that he is with us.

Scripture also forms our way of thinking. It helps us comprehend more deeply who God is and all he has done for us. It helps us adopt God's values.

The Holy Spirit speaks to us in Scripture. As we read, the Lord will guide us, comfort us, and help us.

Commit to reading Scriptures every day. Reflect on what you read!

Perhaps a passage will lead you to thank God for your blessings or deepen your realization that God is in charge and that he is good.

Let Scripture inspire you, that God might "birth" something new in your life.

"Lord, give me a deeper hunger for your word."

June 18

Teach me wisdom and knowledge. (Psalm 119:66)

However much we know about God, there is always more we can learn. We know that he is all-wise, the source of all truth and goodness. We know that he is loving and compassionate. His majesty is beyond our comprehension.

The best way to know about God is to come to know him personally. When you know someone personally, you know much more than data. You know how he feels about things, what makes him sad or happy, and what he thinks about you—because you matter to him and because he shares his heart with you.

That's why God invites us to sit quietly with him every day and ponder his word. As we sit in wonder at God and his beautiful creation, we'll hear his still, small voice whispering words of love, wisdom, and guidance.

So try to sit still today. Accept God's invitation to read Scripture and pray. Delight in the Lord, and seek to know him more. Let him teach you his wisdom. Let him fill you up!

"Lord, as I sit quietly with you today, let me know more of who you are!"

June 19

You did not receive a spirit of slavery to fall back into fear, but you received a spirit of adoption, through which we cry, "Abba, Father!" (Romans 8:15)

The opposites of slavery and fear are freedom and courage, so shouldn't Paul say we receive those spirits? What does "a spirit of adoption" have to do with this?

Everything! We have been adopted as the children of God. The chains of sin are too strong for us to break on our own. Likewise, our courage doesn't come from an excess of grit and determination. Both freedom and courage come from our identity in the Lord. We belong to him, and that knowledge sets us free and encourages us.

That spirit of adoption reminds us that our Father listens to us. So call out to God for help whenever you feel threatened, weary, or scared. Tune in to the witness of the Spirit, so that every day you can become more deeply aware of your adoption—and freer and more courageous as a result.

"Holy Spirit, thank you for calling me a child of God. Remind me today to live with the confidence and freedom of one adopted into his family."

June 20

I have come not to abolish but to fulfill. (Matthew 5:17)

Some people in Jesus' time were so focused on rules and traditions that they lost sight of the big picture. Indeed, they did not recognize that Jesus was the fulfillment of the Law, the Law of God incarnate!

Jesus brought the Law to life. No longer just a series of writings, the Law was a living reality that everyone could experience!

So how do you fulfill the Law? By meticulously keeping every stricture in the Bible? Not exactly. Scripture makes it clear that we fulfill God's commandments through the Holy Spirit. The Spirit writes the Law on our hearts, makes us want to live according to God's ways, and gives us grace to overcome the pull of sin. It is the Spirit—speaking to us through Scripture, our conscience, and fellow believers—who gives us a grasp of the Christian life.

"Come, Holy Spirit, and open my eyes to the glory of the Lord. Teach me and empower me to follow your ways."

June 21

How is it that you came in here without a
wedding garment? (Matthew 22:12)

We can sometimes wonder, *Am I going to have a place in God's kingdom?* Jesus' parable reminds us that we are all invited to God's banquet hall, "bad and good alike" (Matthew 22:10). But we need to be dressed appropriately for this great feast.

What does it mean to be dressed appropriately for heaven?

Our host, God, knows where we are coming from, and he is ready and waiting to supply us with the proper garments—at his expense! We in turn need to wear these garments; we need to choose to clothe ourselves in Jesus Christ by adopting his way of life.

It can be tempting to stick with our own "clothing," to choose self-reliance over faith. But that would be like showing up at a posh dinner dressed in blue jeans and a wrinkled T-shirt! We need to change our clothing!

Accept God's gracious invitation, and ask him to build anticipation for heaven in your heart. Then "put on the Lord Jesus Christ" (Romans 13:14), and prepare to celebrate the wedding feast of the Lamb!

"Lord, clothe me in your wedding garment, and bring me to the feast!"

June 22

Do not be amazed. (John 3:7)

But Nicodemus was amazed! Jesus told him that he had to be "born from above" (John 3:3).

What did that mean?

Being "born from above" means that the Holy Spirit lives in us—ready to encourage us, convict us of sin, fill us with peace, and stir us to do his will. It means that we can be led by the Spirit rather than the desires and drives of our fallen nature. Thus we begin to think as Jesus thinks (see 1 Corinthians 2:16).

Being "born from above" means becoming different—at least from the world's perspective. The Spirit can teach us to look on an offender as someone created by God and equally loved by him. He can teach us to forgive quickly, to discern good from evil, and to be ready to serve.

People will notice the difference in you as you follow the Lord—and they will be intrigued. Seeing how you live a different set of standards might make them more receptive to the good news of Christ.

"Lord, open my spiritual eyes. Holy Spirit, I need more of you today."

June 23

If God is for us, who can be against us? (Romans 8:31)

Chapter 8 of Romans is like a summary—a rousing conclusion—of the gospel message.

1. We are beloved children of God. The Holy Spirit works to convince us that we belong to God. God is for us just as much as a father is for his children.

2. The Holy Spirit "comes to the aid of our weakness" (Romans 8:26). Even in our lowest moments, God is with us, offering us his strength, his guidance, and his consolation.

3. God sent his only Son to save us. This is the clearest evidence of how God loves us and wants us to be by his side.

It's not always easy to trust in these words, but they are true. Yes, your heavenly Father is on your side. Rejoice in this awesome truth!

"Father, you are my hope, my joy, and my strength! I will believe in you today!"

June 24

Pray in the holy Spirit. (Jude 20)

What good advice! When you hear this, you might think about asking the Holy Spirit to help you intercede when you don't know how to pray. But there's more to praying in the Spirit.

How about listening to the Spirit's guidance?

Ask the Spirit to help you review the upcoming day. What will you be doing? Whom will you see? What challenges await you? Pray, "Come, Holy Spirit, and help me see my day through your eyes."

Then listen. You might get a sense that a certain meeting should be postponed. Or that you should reach out to an old friend. Try to act on any sense you receive—especially if it is accompanied by a feeling of peace.

Take opportunities throughout the day to invite the Holy Spirit into your activities. Receive his wisdom about what does not go well, and share your joy about good news you receive.

Interact with the Holy Spirit as you would with a good friend. Let your friendship with him grow!

"Come, Holy Spirit! Walk with me today. Guide me. Help me hear you and follow your lead."

June 25

Then the LORD answered me. (Habakkuk 2:2)

The prophet Habakkuk was about to be engaged in one of the most amazing conversations in the Bible. He was upset with God and wanted to know how God was going to fix the problem. It didn't start out amazing, but ended up filling him with hope.

Do you believe that you can hear God speaking to you? You can, you know. God loves talking with his children. You might begin by coming to God with questions that are on your heart such as, "Why do bad things happen to good people?" Don't be afraid to pour out your heart to him.

Be persistent but patient as well. Watch to see what he will say to you and what answer he will give to your complaint. Sometimes it isn't enough just to make one simple request. Keep on asking. Keep on listening too, trying to discern God's voice among all the other voices in and around you. Devotion to prayer is important if only because friendship takes time!

Finally, write down your thoughts so you don't forget or confuse them. It may take time to see God's plan unfold.

God loves talking with his children, and he wants us to hear him!

"Lord, help me hear your voice. I want to know friendship with you!"

June 26

*[Jesus] addressed . . . those who were convinced
of their own righteousness. (Luke 18:9)*

How do we grow in humility? The virtue of humility is best understood as true knowledge: to see yourself as you really are, neither too high nor too low. If you have an inflated opinion of yourself and look down on other people, humility reminds you that you are a sinner in need of God's mercy. If you have a negative self-image, humility corrects that false impression and acknowledges God's profound love for you and the fact that you are created in his image.

The Pharisee in Jesus' parable led an exemplary life: he was not greedy, dishonest, or adulterous. And yet his prayer did not humble him or open him up to God. The tax collector had an honest appraisal of himself, "a sinner," and his prayer was a real turning toward God: "Be merciful to me" (Luke 18:13).

We are sinners in need of God's love, but we are also deeply loved and valued by God—to the point that Jesus gave his very life for us.

"O God, have mercy on me, a sinner."

June 27

It came through a revelation. (Galatians 1:12)

One of the great joys in life is receiving revelation from God—the sense of his presence and the leading of his Holy Spirit. We can experience this as we make time for God. Scripture tells us to fill our minds with God's word and to meditate on his unfailing love (see Psalm 48:10), his mighty deeds (77:12), his precepts (119:15), and his promises (119:148).

Jesus thanked his Father for having "hidden . . . things from the wise and the learned" and "revealed them to the childlike" (Matthew 11:25). So aim to be childlike in your prayer: trusting, uncomplicated, teachable, and content with little things.

God wants to reveal himself to you. He wants to show you how much he loves you. He wants to guide you in the quiet of your heart—perhaps asking you to be more generous or to speak to that lonely person you just walked past or to have a heart for the poor.

The more we come to God, the more we will hear his voice.

"Jesus, imprint your word on my heart. I want to know your will."

June 28

The word of God is living and effective, sharper than any two-edged sword, . . . able to discern reflections and thoughts of the heart. (Hebrews 4:12)

How is the word of God like this? If we read Scripture stories reflectively, placing ourselves in the situation and testing our reactions, we can learn much about "the reflections and thoughts" that lie buried in our hearts. Dare we allow the Spirit to expose greed, glory seeking, envy, or cold duty, where we would prefer to see prudence, self-esteem, truthfulness, or love?

God knows us through and through, and he still loves us. He offers forgiveness for sin and the power to be transformed.

The same word of God that reveals our deepest thoughts also reveals the Son of God, the powerful high priest who understands our every burden and temptation. "So let us confidently approach the throne of grace to receive mercy and to find grace for timely help" (Hebrews 4:16).

"Jesus, Word of God, search my heart and know my thoughts. I come to you just as I am, eager to encounter you."

June 29

*Be holy, for I, the L*ORD *your God, am holy.*
(Leviticus 19:2)

Yes, God is the model of holiness: pure, powerful, majestic, perfect. And underpinning all these attributes is the deepest, most selfless love we can imagine. From the moment of creation to the giving of his only Son to right now, God pours himself out for us, holding nothing back.

As we encounter God's love, we change. You've probably seen it in your own life. When you experience God's mercy, your heart becomes more tender toward others. When you spend time in prayer, you become more patient and gentler.

But don't be discouraged if you aren't perfectly loving right now. Growing in holiness is about letting God's love shape you over time.

Invite God into your interactions with your family, your coworkers, your boss, your neighbors. Ask him to show you how you can love people better.

As you go about your day, pray this simple prayer: "Lord, use me." Then watch how he nudges you here and there to give more of yourself to the people around you. That's how he makes you holy!

"Lord, use me."

June 30

Blessed be the God and Father of our Lord Jesus Christ,
who has blessed us in Christ with every spiritual
blessing in the heavens, as he chose us in him, before
the foundation of the world, to be holy and without
blemish before him. (Ephesians 1:3-4)

These words fill the Christian heart with hope and gratitude. God Almighty, the Creator and Ruler of the universe, loves us personally and has given us all we need to fulfill his purposes here on earth and into eternity.

Think of it. Before God created a single thing, he had you in mind. Before you said or did anything, he fashioned you with the capacity to be filled with his divine life.

When we fail to live up to the great gifts we have been given, we can turn to the Father in repentance. He will forgive us and comfort us. He will strengthen us and give us an even deeper foretaste of the life we will experience with him in eternity.

In your prayer today, ask the Spirit, "What do you want to show me today?" Then, ask him to give you a deeper sense of awe at your heavenly inheritance.

"Thank you, Father, for choosing me to be your beloved
child. May I always remain faithful to your calling."

July

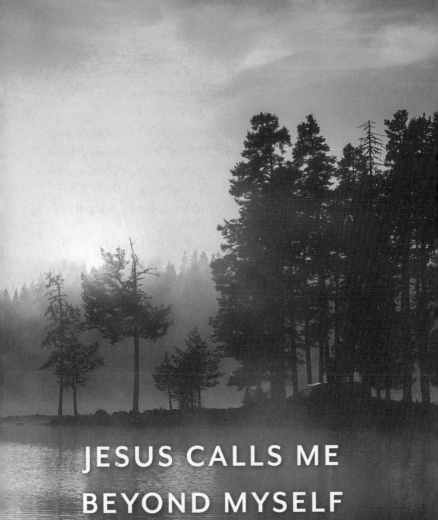

JESUS CALLS ME
BEYOND MYSELF

July 1

[Samuel] ran to Eli and said, "Here I am." (1 Samuel 3:5)

The story of the young Samuel responding to God's voice has three pieces of encouraging news for us.

First, it's okay to struggle. Samuel didn't recognize God's voice at first. We too are still learning how to tune in to the Spirit. Second, God is patient with his people, sending us messages even though we will likely miss some of them. Finally, you're probably hearing from the Lord already without realizing it.

Why did Samuel run to Eli when God called him? Perhaps God's voice sounded so "natural" that Samuel looked for a natural source.

God often chooses natural means to speak to us, including our consciences, imaginations, thoughts, and feelings. Keep that in mind as you pray. If you feel your heart moved by a phrase of Scripture, take note. If someone's name pops into your mind, perhaps you should pray for the person and seek ways to encourage them.

The Lord will speak to you. Trust that he will give you ears to hear his voice.

"Lord, I'm honored that you speak to me. Help me tune in to what you're saying."

July 2

I did just as I was commanded. (Ezekiel 12:7)

Throughout the Old Testament, messengers were sent to call people back to the Lord. Ezekiel carried God's message in an unusual way: he acted it out. As God said to him, "I am making you a sign for the house of Israel" (Ezekiel 12:6).

Today there are millions of believers living out the prophetic message of God, telling others about the Father's love and the promise of redemption.

Did you know that you too are a prophet?

You have the Holy Spirit, the Spirit of Christ, in you, and that Spirit is capable of making you into a messenger of the gospel.

You don't have to do anything unusual. Just try your best to follow the Lord, and you'll stand out. Your kindness and compassion will strike a chord in people. Your decision to sacrifice time and energy to help someone sends a message about God's constant care for his people. Your patience and forgiveness can melt someone's heart.

You are a prophetic presence in this world, a messenger for Christ.

"Lord, let me spread your word today and always."

July 3

Joseph . . . did as the angel of the Lord had commanded.
(Matthew 1:24)

Joseph's yes to God was important. It made him the foster father of Jesus, and it gave us a moving portrait of what trust and faith look like.

Our decisions might not be as consequential as Joseph's was, but each involves embracing one future and closing the door to other possibilities. Every time we say yes to God, we take a step along the path he has for us—a path that leads us to heaven. And God says yes right back to us, filling us with his grace, assuring us of his presence, making us more like his Son, Jesus.

Joseph, a "righteous man," probably said yes to the Lord in his carpentry business, in the town square, and in the secret places of his heart (Matthew 1:19). Each decision strengthened him in saying yes to God. So too, our daily yeses to God can prepare us for the bigger things he may ask of us.

Never forget: every yes to God is filled with power and grace.

"Lord, help me stay faithful in the small things, so that I can follow you wherever you lead me."

July 4

He appointed twelve [whom he also named apostles]
that they might be with him. (Mark 3:14)

When Jesus chose his apostles, he picked people whom he could trust to heal and preach on his behalf. They had to know Jesus well, to learn not only his thoughts and plans but also his desires and dreams. They had to know what was on his heart. And so Jesus wanted these men to "be with him."

There are many ways we can get to know Jesus better; one is to spend time every day reading and studying Scripture. We can take what we learn there, come before the Lord, and ask him about some of the issues we face: personally, in our community, and in the world around us. His word guides us as we seek answers and opens us to the Holy Spirit's leading to new areas of discipleship.

The more we know Jesus and how he thinks and feels, the better apostles we will be.

"Jesus, thank you for choosing me to follow you. Help me know you more deeply so that I can serve you today."

July 5

This is the work of God, that you believe. (John 6:29)

The crowd who followed Jesus were drawn by his miracles. They witnessed healings of the blind, the lame, and the diseased. They were miraculously fed with loaves and fishes. Now Jesus wanted to lead them to faith in him as the Son of God, who gives eternal life to all who believe.

"Believe." This was a hard word for the people to hear. They still wanted earthly signs. They were not ready to face the challenge of faith.

It's not hard to sympathize with this crowd. Faith is not always an easy journey. When life is good and we have lots of signs of God's love, it's easy to believe. But it's in the stormy seas of life that our faith grows.

This is where persistence pays off. Whether you are in good times or hard, press on to grow in your faith. Ask questions, and use your God-given faculty of reason to see the truth of every situation you are in. Your faith will grow.

"Jesus, strengthen the gift of faith that you have given me. Help me persevere in seeking you in all things."

July 6

They did not stop teaching and proclaiming the Messiah.
(Acts 5:42)

The power of God is certainly greater than anything man-made. And Christianity is more than just a set of ideas. It is "the power of God for the salvation of everyone who believes" (Romans 1:16). The dynamic message of the gospel reaches into hearts and lives and changes people from the inside out.

That's true for you as well as the people in your life who don't yet believe in Christ!

Don't shortchange yourself—or God, for that matter—by thinking that only extra-holy people can be effective witnesses for Christ. If you can find an opportunity today to share something about your faith, you will make a difference.

It's not about you anyway; it's about Jesus and his power! Surely you can rely on him as you share your story. And when you do, know that it's not just you speaking. The Holy Spirit is there in your words, adding his grace to your witness.

"Lord, may your Spirit shine through me today, making me courageous in bearing witness in all that I say and do."

July 7

She, from her poverty, has contributed all she had,
her whole livelihood. (Mark 12:44)

The Gospels are filled with examples of Jesus' finding solace, strength, and encouragement from women of deep faith: his own mother; Martha and her sister, Mary; Mary Magdalene; and many others. Here this poor widow shows herself to be part of this heroic company!

This woman's paltry gift drew Jesus' admiration. It was all she had to live on, and yet she freely donated it to support the Temple, the grand house of worship. In making this offering, she entrusted herself completely to God. Perhaps her action moved Jesus so much because he stood on the precipice of his own complete offering to God.

We too can inspire Jesus by our trust in God. We can bring joy to his heart by showing him courageous love today. We can give from our substance and not just our surplus, knowing that he meets all our needs.

"Here I am, Lord; let my heart become a resting place for you."

July 8

Offer no resistance to one who is evil. (Matthew 5:39)

This difficult teaching is not one that we can ignore. Jesus didn't avoid it. His steadiness in the face of persecution was remarkable.

"How can I be like that?" we wonder. By loving.

Love kept Jesus going through all the hardships he encountered. Love formed the foundation for everything he said and did. Love made it possible for him to forgive even as he hung on the cross.

Let's ask Jesus to fill us with his heavenly perspective. Maybe we can perform an act of kindness toward someone who has hurt us. We can ask the Holy Spirit for wisdom in relationships we find difficult. Praying for people can help us forgive as we have been forgiven.

How abundant is the grace God is willing to give us! He has poured out his Spirit to make the impossible possible. Our job is to keep trying, "confident of this, that the one who began a good work in [us] will continue to complete it" (Philippians 1:6).

The greatest gift we can give is love.

"Jesus, I want to follow you all the way. I put my trust in you and in your saving power."

July 9

Whoever wishes to come after me must deny himself, take up his cross, and follow me. (Matthew 16:24)

Some historians believe that Jesus' cross could have weighed three hundred pounds. The Romans often had the condemned carry only the crossbeam—which still weighed more than a hundred pounds. When we consider this—not to mention the spiritual and emotional weight that the cross entailed— we can appreciate that Jesus understands our own suffering and challenges. He shared the same sorrows, pains, and weight of the crosses that we bear in our lives.

Jesus' call to take up our crosses and follow him is an invitation to join him and to find our strength in his companionship. He will make our yoke easy and our burden light (see Matthew 11:28-30).

Times of suffering can bring us closer to God, or they can push us further away from him. It's our choice. Staying close to Jesus amid difficulties might not be easy at first, but it will bring us peace and comfort. All we need to do is take that first step.

"Lord, thank you for continuing to come to me when I need help. Thank you for walking alongside me and making my burdens lighter."

July 10

When you fast . . . (Matthew 6:17)

"There is no love more sincere than the love of food." This quote, penned in humor by the Irish playwright George Bernard Shaw, contains a kernel of truth. Not only does food satisfy our physical hunger, but it can bring us comfort and happiness. The idea of intentionally going without it can make us uncomfortable.

Fasting is a valuable spiritual discipline. It gives us more time for prayer. The physical hunger we feel can put us in touch with our spiritual hunger. As Jesus taught, we don't live on bread alone "but by every word that comes forth from the mouth of God" (Matthew 4:4).

Fasting can put us more in touch with God's love, his desires, and his peace. These spiritual rewards far outweigh any temporary feelings of discomfort.

Jesus didn't say "if you fast" but rather "when you fast." Keep it simple at first. Give up one meal, and spend that time focusing on the Lord in prayer or reading Scripture. Try this once a week, and see yourself become more attuned to the Lord!

"Lord Jesus, I'm hungry for your words of life."

July 11

The lamp of the body is the eye. (Matthew 6:22)

Jesus teaches that what we take in through our eyes shapes our hearts and our actions. Think about the many images you absorb each day: through television, magazines, billboards, the Internet, social media.

Do these images dominate your mind?

Do they influence your thoughts and actions?

You can guard your eyes by deciding what you will watch and what you will avoid. Pay attention to what you see. Which images should you filter out, and which are good and upbuilding?

Some images are hard to avoid. Try to catch negative ones before they become part of your thought process. Focusing instead on wholesome and uplifting images can help keep your thoughts pure and full of light, giving you peace and a sense of steadiness.

Here is one foolproof way to make your eyes as clear as possible: fix them "on Jesus, the leader and perfecter of faith" (Hebrews 12:2).

"Lord, help me guard my eyes and turn my heart to you."

July 12

Saul, Saul, why are you persecuting me? (Acts 22:7)

This isn't the first time God has questioned one of his people. God asked Adam and Eve, "Where are you? . . . Who told you that you were naked? Have you eaten from the tree?" (Genesis 3:9, 11). When Elijah took refuge in a cave, God asked, "Why are you here?" (1 Kings 19:9). The risen Jesus asked two disciples on the road to Emmaus, "What are you discussing as you walk along?" (Luke 24:17).

God opened conversations by which people could come face-to-face with their sins, their fears, or their needs.

Jesus might question you too.

What makes you anxious?

What can you do today to build my kingdom?

Whom can you love a little more?

Let Jesus ask, and don't be afraid to answer. Adam and Eve found the promise of restoration, Elijah found the courage to press on, the disciples' eyes were opened to see Jesus, and Saul of Tarsus became a great apostle. Imagine what can happen to you as you hear and answer!

"Thank you, Jesus, for caring enough to ask me how I'm doing."

July 13

Hold fast to the hope that lies before us. This we have as an anchor of the soul, sure and firm. (Hebrews 6:18-19)

Jesus Christ is our "high priest" before God, who intercedes for us (Hebrews 6:20). Hold on to Jesus, the Hebrews author urges. Jesus is steadfast, and he will keep you safe in any storm. He is your anchor, who holds you fast to the mercy and presence of God.

When a boat drifts, the anchor pulls it back. Some days, you might feel that you have drifted away. Be assured, your anchor can hold you! You may feel its tug in a twinge of conscience, a hesitation, a conviction. This tug assures you that Jesus has not abandoned you, that you are still "rooted and grounded" in Christ (Ephesians 3:17).

This anchor "reaches into the interior," right into the presence of God (Hebrews 6:19). Day after day, challenge after challenge, Jesus is with you, interceding for you and making your faith and hope and trust in him firmer. His promises are sure, and his faithfulness is absolute.

"Thank you, Father, for the hope and confidence that your promises give me. Thank you for anchoring me to you!"

July 14

The LORD is with you, you mighty warrior! (Judges 6:12)

A messenger from God tells Gideon to go save Israel, because the Lord is with him!

What do you do when God nudges you forward?

You may find yourself contemplating the past instead of dreaming about the future. You may dwell on the times when things didn't work out and forget all the times God was with you.

"I don't know if anyone I've ever prayed for has been healed, so what's the point?" "Peace with that person would be wonderful, but our relationship is beyond repair." "I've never been able to overcome this habit; why should this time be any different?"

God overflows with patience and kindness toward us. That's why he will sometimes confirm his message. He did this with Gideon three separate times!

The angel's first words to Gideon, "The Lord is with you," allowed him to focus not on his own strength but on God's. Look to God for courage. There's no limit to what he can accomplish through you.

"I have the strength for everything through him who empowers me!" (Philippians 4:13)

July 15

If we live in the Spirit, let us also follow the Spirit.
(Galatians 5:25)

We belong to Christ. Our sinful passions were crucified in Baptism, and we have been filled with the Holy Spirit (see Galatians 5:24).

So why don't we live this way all the time?

The call to holiness is a process; the sinful aspects of our nature don't disappear overnight. God never loses sight of Jesus' sacrifice for us, the life of his Spirit within us, the natural goodness he created in us, or our desires for godliness. He sees it all—and it makes him smile!

Don't be disheartened when you stumble. Don't look just at the temptations that you give in to; look also at the fruit of the Spirit that you demonstrate. Be encouraged at your victories, and ask the Spirit to strengthen you in areas where you are weak. Look to Jesus and to his mighty power.

"Lord, I rejoice in your life in me and in the working of your Holy Spirit to conform me to your image. May my heart be always open to your call."

July 16

Do you have eyes and not see, ears and not hear?
(Mark 8:18)

Perhaps the most common obstacle to listening is thinking that we already know what someone is trying to say, so we don't pay close attention.

It appears that the disciples are guilty of this. After a busy time of ministry and travel, they have their minds on their next meal. When Jesus tries to give them a spiritual warning, they assume he is talking about food!

It can be hard to see things from God's perspective, to hear what he wants to say to us. Like the disciples, we can focus instead on our needs and problems. Of course, God is concerned with our daily needs, and he wants us to bring them to him. But that is not the only thing we do in prayer.

God wants to reveal his mind to us, to share his thoughts with us. This is a great privilege, something to treasure every day!

Listen to God. It's not easy; sometimes we hear silence! But if we make the space, God will speak. He has much to say to us.

"Lord, give me ears to hear your voice."

July 17

*His heart was moved . . . ; and he began
to teach them many things. (Mark 6:34)*

The apostles returned from a very successful mission trip:
they had healed people, delivered others from demons,
and brought many to conversion. Jesus invited them to get
away for a time of rest (see Mark 6:31). But a crowd of people
followed, and Jesus changed his plans. You could say that the
"practical" Jesus was overcome by the "compassionate" Jesus.

Jesus wants us to take care of ourselves, but there are times
when he wants us to put our plans aside for the greater good.

You may receive a prompting to speak to someone after
church or in the grocery store. You may feel that God wants
you to hug your husband or child or sit down and read Scripture for a few minutes. As you act on such compassionate
movements from God, you will grow in your ability to recognize them and truly be his disciple.

*"Jesus, help me sense your Spirit's promptings and follow
your leadings."*

July 18

Speak, L ORD, for your servant is listening. (1 Samuel 3:9)

When we first experience the presence of the Lord, we can be in awe over the fact that we can rush to him and tell him of our needs, fears, and problems, as well as our gratitude and joy. We might tend to do a lot of talking and asking, in effect saying, "Listen, Lord, your servant is speaking."

As we grow in our prayer life, we spend less time speaking and more time listening. We find joy simply by being in God's presence; we feel awe, and we worship him for who he is. We savor his words and ponder them in the depths of our hearts. We let him change us rather than trying to get him to change our circumstances.

God longs to speak to us. Let us be attentive to him as we pray, read Scripture, or listen to an inspiring talk. His peace, his joy, and his love will flow.

"Lord, speak your words of truth to me, so that I may know you, serve you, and bear fruit for the kingdom of God."

July 19

Great crowds . . . followed him. (Matthew 4:25)

Of course great crowds followed Jesus: he was magnetic! Everyone who encountered him went away with renewed hope, joy, and a sense of freedom.

Jesus is calling you and empowering you to be a spiritual magnet as well. When you sit with him in private prayer or worship him with brothers and sisters in Christ, he fills you with his love so that you can give it away. He wants you to bring light to people in the shadows, healing to people who are hurting, and hope to people in despair.

The Spirit in you is contagious, reaching out to people and opening their hearts to the Lord. As you grow in the Lord, you will find yourself sharing your faith more easily and perhaps even praying with people for healing. Strangers might walk up and ask why you look so happy!

You can be a magnet for Christ. Answer his call!

"Here I am, Jesus. Fill me with your life as I spend time with you each day, and let this life flow to others."

July 20

Talitha koum, . . . Little girl, I say to you, arise!
(Mark 5:41)

Imagine yourself as the lifeless girl, lying in a bed of nothingness. Two words break into your darkness: *"Talitha koum!"* Jesus is speaking to you alone.

Then you notice that he is holding your hand. And Jesus is smiling at you. With a firm love he is telling you, arise! Power flows from him, enabling you to get up from your deathbed.

God often tells his servants to arise. He told Elijah, "Arise, go to Zarephath" (1 Kings 17:9). He told a dead man, "Young man, I tell you, arise!" (Luke 7:14). *Get up! I have a plan for you!*

Today during your prayer, stand up straight and tall. Ask God what he wants you to do next. Don't worry if it sounds impossible. Just keep your eyes "fixed on Jesus" (Hebrews 12:2). He can raise the dead; he can surely lead you!

"Jesus, I stand ready to do whatever you call me to."

July 21

If you greet your brothers only,
what is unusual about that? (Matthew 5:47)

We naturally love people who love us. Mosaic Law encouraged the Israelites to go a bit further and love their brethren. God goes even further: his love extends to those who don't love him at all.

Jesus urges us to love unconditionally, as he did from the cross. You might wonder, *How can I do that?*

As we become immersed in God's tenderness and mercy, barriers in our relationships will break down. Our hearts will soften. We will want to treat people the way God treats us. And that will make us stretch outside our everyday boundaries and reach out to people.

Let us show the world what a disciple of Christ is. Jesus promised that people will know we belong to him because of the way we love (see John 13:35).

Talk to someone you don't know. You might feel uncomfortable at first, but that's okay. When you take that first step, God will surprise you. You might recognize God's presence in someone and start to love as God loves!

"Lord, help me be 'unusual' today."

July 22

God raised this Jesus; of this we are all witnesses.
(Acts 2:32)

Peter was excited because something new and wonderful had touched his life: God raised Jesus from the dead, and Peter was among the witnesses! And then Peter discovered the power in the message of the gospel, as "about three thousand persons were added," and "many wonders and signs were done through the apostles" (Acts 2:41, 43).

As Jesus touches our lives, we feel compelled to share our hope and excitement with the people around us. And the more we step out of our comfort zones to talk about Jesus, the more excited we become. Why? We see people's lives change as they hear about Jesus—even if his message comes from everyday people like us.

Tell people about God's love. Tell them how Jesus' resurrection can overcome fear and sin in them. People are longing for the truth—and you can give it to them!

"Jesus, risen Lord, give me the boldness to share the good news of your victory today. Help me proclaim that you are our best and brightest hope!"

July 23

What must I do to be saved? (Acts 16:30)

Jailed for preaching and performing miracles in the name of Jesus, Paul and Silas praised God at the top of their voices. Jesus was still the Lord, and his plan was moving forward. Suddenly an earthquake broke their chains and opened the prison doors.

The presence of Christ in these men was as striking as God's dramatic intervention to free them. Their jailer fell to his knees and asked to know the Lord, and the disciples forgave him and enabled him to experience God's forgiveness. They cared more for him than for their own safety.

In the face of injustice or in the midst of a struggle, we can maintain our peace in the Lord. Often the way we hold our ground strikes people far more than the words we speak.

Is God working through you? If you listen closely to him and hold on to your joy, your love and peace may make a difference in someone's life.

"Lord, still my anxiety, and help me listen for your gentle direction."

July 24

Be merciful. (Luke 6:36)

Jesus said, "Forgive and you will be forgiven" (Luke 6:37). In other words, we can't expect God to forgive us if we aren't willing to forgive other people.

It's difficult to let go of past hurts! Should we forgive those who don't apologize, who won't acknowledge their actions, who are too self-absorbed to be aware of the hurt they have caused?

Yes. Mercy is a free gift we give to someone out of loving kindness, not because the recipient earns it. It comes from a generous heart.

To forgive someone who has wronged you is one of the greatest gifts you can give Jesus. It's also a powerful sign of God's kingdom on earth.

So ask the Holy Spirit to make you merciful. He will empower you to speak words of forgiveness even before you fully mean them. He can bring you to the point of forgiving so genuinely that you'll be able to smile at the mention of the person's name.

You can be merciful as your heavenly Father is merciful!

"Holy Spirit, let my heart bathe in your love and overflow with mercy toward others."

July 25

The Son of Man did not come to be served but to serve.
(Matthew 20:28)

J esus offers us an invitation to be like him: to become the least, so that we can become the greatest servants of the Lord.

Do you want a good place in heaven?

Then start by taking the lowest place on earth. Be a servant in your home. Seek to give rather than receive, to love rather than be loved. Volunteer in your parish or community. Your options are wide open.

If you are already serving and giving, there may be ground to be gained in your attitude while you are serving. Ask the Holy Spirit to help you take on a servant's heart. Jesus will bless every effort you make. He will lift you up and fill you with his love and grace!

"Jesus, change my heart to be more like yours. I want to serve rather than be served and to love rather than be loved. Let me be last, so that you and your gospel may be first in my life."

July 26

*Elisha left the oxen, ran after Elijah, and said,
"Please, let me kiss my father and mother good-bye,
and I will follow you." (1 Kings 19:20)*

Elisha was so certain that God was calling him that he burned the tools of his trade and sacrificed his oxen. He didn't know what the future held, but he trusted that the Lord would provide. His story tells us that sometimes we need to make a break with the old in order to enter a new season of fruitfulness.

Transitions can require sacrifices: leaving home to get married, leaving one job for another, or simply making a new friend can entail leaving behind some aspect of our "old life." We can trust that God will walk with us across the threshold into that something new. Because God is with us, we can take that step in faith.

When a change involving sacrifice comes up in your life, think of Elisha and his burning equipment. Offer yourself to the Lord. Put your life and your gifts at his service. Every offering brings a smile to his face.

*"Here I am, Jesus, ready for whatever you have in store
for me."*

July 27

Without parables he did not speak to them. (Mark 4:34)

Mark tells us that Jesus spoke in parables to the people around him, mystifying even his closest disciples. Part of his strategy was to provoke his listeners to think more deeply about God and about their lives. He wanted to awaken in them a hunger for God. Then, when they were ready, he could open their hearts to the "mystery of the kingdom of God" (Mark 4:11).

You might be a mystery to many people. The fact that you read Scripture, pray, and go to church on Sunday might strike them as odd. And hopefully you forgive people from the heart—or at least try to.

Do you try to see God in the people around you?

Of course, you're not so strange. You're only doing what God created you to do: love him and love your neighbor.

So keep being quirky! Love. Forgive. Pray. Give. Try to be like Jesus. In doing so, you may win others to him.

"Jesus, help me reflect your love today."

July 28

Do not worry about how you are to speak.
(Matthew 10:19)

Jesus told his disciples not to worry when they faced road-blocks such as being handed over to courts or punished in synagogues. Nowadays he might caution against anxiety when we face apathy, secularism, or relativism.

Do we have what it takes to spread the gospel?

Jesus wants us to put aside any worry, because speaking his word is not about us! It doesn't depend on the strength of our personality, the depth of our intellect, or our oratorical skills. The Spirit will overcome what we lack. All Jesus asks is that we use the opportunities that come our way.

With the heart of an evangelist, you can pass on the amazing gift you have received. Just open your mouth and speak, assured that it will be "the Spirit of your Father speaking through you" (Matthew 10:20).

"Jesus, you want everyone to receive the awesome gift of your redemption. Help me put away worry, so that your life can flow out of me and touch the people you put in my path."

July 29

*He made a whip of cords and drove them
all out of the temple area. (John 2:15)*

Was Jesus angry? Elsewhere he said, "Whoever is angry with his brother will be liable to judgment" (Matthew 5:22).

There is a type of anger that isn't sinful. In fact, there are times when anger is an appropriate response to injustice. We have a right to be angry at abortion, racism, sexual abuse, and child trafficking.

Paul said, "Be angry but do not sin" (Ephesians 4:26). We need to control anger by reason and compassion. We must not let it overpower us or overshadow the call to love and forgive. Jesus' anger was controlled, for immediately after clearing the Temple, he continued his ministry of preaching and teaching with calmness, conviction, and clarity.

Be vigilant in keeping your emotions under control, linking your reactions to good reason, love, and humility. And once you have said your piece about an injustice, try to resolve the situation and restore love and trust.

"Jesus, teach me how to be angry without sinning."

July 30

Unless your righteousness surpasses that of the scribes and
Pharisees, you will not enter into the kingdom of heaven.
(Matthew 5:20)

Jesus dramatically elevated the standards for his disciples to live by. They were to heed even "the least of these commandments" (Matthew 5:19). He went on to expand the commandment against murder to include injunctions against speaking and even thinking violence against others.

Why such a high standard, beyond the law given to Moses and the prophets? Because it's a true reflection of the Father's heart. God wants to raise his people to a greater conformity to his own character. And as the stakes are raised, we become more alert to our need for his grace. Holiness is impossible by ourselves!

Is Jesus inviting you to dive deeper in your friendship with him?

What Jesus asks you to do may feel impossible. But you're not on your own; the Holy Spirit is with you. Rely on him, and you may find yourself doing the impossible!

"Jesus, I hear you calling me. Please help me answer."

July 31

Those who were ready went into the wedding feast.
(Matthew 25:10)

The parable of the ten virgins urges us to be alert and awake, ready for the time when Jesus will come again. Whether it's referring to enough oil for a lamp as with the virgins, or referring to us with our faith or the Holy Spirit or the grace of God; it's something that we can't borrow from a friend; we have to be prepared with our own supply. How much we have will determine whether we are ready or not when Jesus comes.

Jesus wants us to keep our faith alive every single day.

How? We can take our cue from St. Paul: "If you confess with your mouth that Jesus is Lord and believe in your heart that God raised him from the dead, you will be saved" (Romans 10:9).

We have a prime opportunity to check our faith every day in our personal prayer. We can be sure that whenever we confess and believe, we bring a smile to God's face. We can hear the angels announce, "Behold, the bridegroom! Come out to meet him!" (Matthew 25:6).

"Jesus, I believe in you."

Notes

August

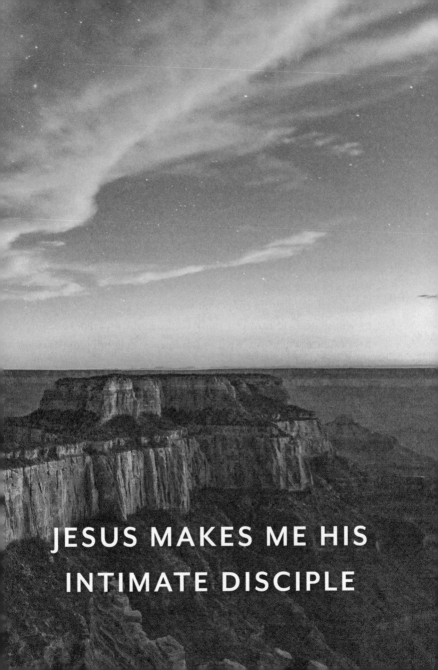

JESUS MAKES ME HIS
INTIMATE DISCIPLE

August 1

Those who offer praise as a sacrifice honor me.
(Psalm 50:23)

We all have obligations: driving kids to school, staying late at the office to finish a project, paying bills. These everyday duties can seem monotonous and "unspiritual." But we can intentionally praise the Lord amid our activities.

This isn't always easy; that's why the psalmist called it a sacrifice. Sometimes we may not want to turn to the Lord, lest he ask something of us that we don't want to give. But as we invite God into our daily routine, our awareness of his presence will grow. We'll find ourselves delighting in the Lord and his love.

Take time to tell God how much you love him and want to glorify him. Then try your best to welcome him into your daily situations. Talk with him about the traffic while you're driving and about the meal you're planning for your family. You can even complain to him about a deadline at work and ask for his help. The more you do this, the more it will become second nature to you.

You will find yourself praising God all the time!

"Lord, teach me to welcome you into my activities today."

August 2

It is the spirit that gives life. (John 6:63)

Jesus often left his followers wondering just what he meant in his parables. Like when he seemed to tell them to use their money to buy friends (see Luke 16:9) or told them that they must eat his flesh and drink his blood (see John 6:53-58). The disciples were confused when they heard these words, but they were convinced that Jesus was "the Holy One of God" (John 6:69). That helped them hold on when they didn't understand fully.

Sometimes you just need a good teacher. Can you remember a teacher in your life that gave you clarity on a subject in a way no other teacher had been able to?

We might come across Scripture passages that aren't easy to understand. We need a good, patient teacher. We need the Holy Spirit. That's the time to follow the disciples' lead and ask the Spirit to teach us.

The Holy Spirit works in many ways—in Scripture, through our consciences, through other people in our lives. In all of these, the key ingredient is our humble, trusting response. Like Peter, we know that Jesus has "the words of eternal life" (John 6:68).

"Holy Spirit, open my heart to the life-giving words of Jesus."

August 3

The word of God continued to spread and grow.
(Acts 12:24)

The Holy Spirit fell upon the 120 gathered at Pentecost, enabling them to proclaim the wonders of God in many languages. The apostles worked miracles. Thousands heard the word of God and believed. And two thousand years later, Christians across the globe bear witness to the power and love of God in their lives.

God wants to use you to spread his word and his love across the world! He promises that his word will never return to him empty but will accomplish the purposes for which he sends it (see Isaiah 55:10-11). Every opportunity you take to share your faith will be blessed.

What opportunities in your daily life do you have to evangelize?

You may see a person come to instant conversion. You may simply plant a seed or water a seed that someone else has planted. God works through it all. He is even more eager than you to see people embrace the gospel!

"Lord, give me the courage to tell of your love to those I meet. Teach me how to offer hope to those who need the light of Christ."

August 4

Mary has chosen the better part. (Luke 10:42)

Martha loved Jesus deeply and expressed that love by making a fine meal for him. But she was so busy making the evening "perfect" that she didn't spend any time with her guest.

"Lord, do you not care that my sister has left me by myself to do the serving?" (Luke 10:40). Martha expressed a self-concern that was robbing her of the precious gift of Jesus' presence. At the same time, these words show how comfortable she was with him. Martha knew where to go when she was upset—directly to Jesus!

Jesus' gentle rebuke was meant to help Martha recognize how needless her anxiety was. He appreciated her loving care, but she really needed to enjoy his company. He had come to be with her and her sister, not to have an elaborate meal!

When you're occupied with the necessary tasks of daily life, try your best to serve with love, as Martha did. But also be careful to keep your eyes on Jesus.

"Jesus, come be my guest! I want to welcome you into my heart and make a home for you there."

August 5

For Zion's sake I will not be silent,
for Jerusalem's sake I will not keep still. (Isaiah 62:1)

God doesn't want us to be silent, shy, or self-absorbed when it comes to our faith. He needs us to bear the good news confidently to this troubled world.

Does this sound daunting?

Don't worry. God sees your weaknesses, your fears, and your concerns, and yet he calls you "My Delight" (Isaiah 62:4). He rejoices over you and showers you with the grace to rise above your limitations.

Jesus sees the state of the world—the sadness, pain, and division. Jesus asks all of us, "Will you feed my sheep? Will you be my light to the world? Will you answer my call to evangelize?"

Jesus could do it himself—and sometimes he does. But nothing gives him more joy than seeing us stand up and say—in both word and deed—"Jesus loves you. Come with me and see what he can do in your life."

"Lord, give me the strength to be your light to the world. Help me grow in confidence. Lord, I want to serve you!"

August 6

Follow me, and let the dead bury their dead.
(Matthew 8:22)

Jesus issues the ultimate challenge of discipleship. He isn't telling us to abandon our families. No, he wants us to release things—or thoughts—that hold us back from living fully with him.

The disciples left their homes, but they had a harder time letting go of their prejudices against Samaritans, their perceptions of Gentiles, and their desires to sit on thrones of power. Abandoning those thought patterns brought them a new joyous life in Christ—the radiant joy that became a trademark of the early Church.

Think about what things or ideas you need to release so that you can take one step closer to becoming more like Jesus. Ask the Spirit to show you any prejudice, anger, or material possessions that hold you back from following God's plans for your life. Loosen your grip on just one thing, and let your heart experience the freedom and joy God has for you!

"Lord, help me let go of anything that inhibits my ability to love you. I want to follow your plans for my life."

August 7

Lord, if it is you, command me to come to you.
(Matthew 14:28)

From the moment Peter abandoned his fishing nets, he followed Jesus wherever he went and tried to imitate him. Peter even got out of a boat and tried to walk on water! He had to be where Jesus was.

Peter promised at the Last Supper that he would never deny Jesus. But just as he floundered in the water, Peter gave in to fear a few hours after his promise—denying Jesus three times. Jesus again rescued Peter, this time with a single glance (see Luke 22:61). That look made Peter aware of his sin and led him to a realization of his weakness and need for forgiveness. Jesus' love gave Peter the courage to keep trying to follow the Lord.

Peter knew he wasn't perfect. He kept his eyes on Jesus and persisted in taking each next step toward him. Jesus' love had set his heart ablaze, and that fire continued to burn because Peter didn't give up.

Look into Jesus' eyes, and receive his gentle look of love. Let your heart burn with that love.

"Lord, enkindle in me a desire to follow you and remain close to you my whole life."

August 8

Come after me, and I will make you fishers of men.
(Mark 1:17)

Our decision to follow Jesus is not a onetime choice. No matter how mature our yes to Jesus is, the Holy Spirit wants to take it to a deeper level. He wants to help us mature in our commitment to him, so that we can know him better and become more effective servants of his kingdom.

This principle applies also to our call to help other people follow Jesus. Our children and friends might immediately take our advice and give their lives to the Lord, but many will need more than one simple invitation. We need to be consistent in mirroring Jesus to them: showing them love, caring for them, telling them that Jesus is all about love and mercy, redemption and reconciliation.

Jesus is calling you to follow him today. He is asking you to keep evangelizing people with love and compassion. It's a challenging call; don't even try to do it alone. Jesus has all the grace you need to evangelize with words, actions, or both.

Maybe people will see the "fire" in you today and say, "I want what you have!"

"Lord, I will follow you all the days of my life."

August 9

Lay your hand on her, and she will live. (Matthew 9:18)

We need human contact as much as we need verbal affirmation to assure us that we are loved. God also communicates through physical touch. Jesus took the sick girl "by the hand" and called to her (Matthew 9:25).

The healing touch of God continued with the apostles, who received the Holy Spirit at Pentecost. The Book of Acts shows Peter, Paul, and the other apostles bringing healing and deliverance as they touched people.

We have the same Spirit! He gives divine life to our souls and to our bodies (see Romans 8:11). That means that everything we do can be sanctified, and everyone we interact with can receive that Spirit too!

You have something to offer anyone who is troubled, afraid, or discouraged. A touch on the shoulder, a pat on the back, or a warm hug can be powerful. Christ is in you, using your hands to touch people, your eyes to see needs, your presence to heal.

"Lord, fill me with your peace, so I can be your presence in this troubled world. Show me how I can touch people with your love and mercy."

August 10

[Jesus] said to him, "See that you tell no one anything." . . . The man went away and began to publicize the whole matter. (Mark 1:44, 45)

Why did Jesus order the healed leper to conceal this miracle? It's been suggested that he wanted to give us an example: like Jesus, we should yearn to remain concealed in the great things that we do. Jesus' motive was simply love, not the limelight.

Yet the good that Jesus does should come to light for the good of others. Testifying to his grace is often the holiest response we can make when God helps us or does something wonderful through us. We must be sure to emphasize God's role in the story.

What you say may inspire someone to turn to the Lord. That's how the people who heard about the leper's healing responded. They streamed out of their towns to find Jesus in the wilderness.

Sharing what God has done for you can seem risky, but the reward can be sweet for the people around you. Maybe they too will find Jesus in their wilderness.

"Lord, I need healing. Reach out and give me your servant's heart."

August 11

The house was filled with the fragrance of the oil.
(John 12:3)

Jesus' friend Mary's gift of spikenard, a type of perfumed oil, reveals extravagant devotion, not only because of how much it cost but because of how she gave it. In an act of adoration and worship, she anointed Jesus' feet. She took on the position of a household servant, who had the job of washing the feet of guests as they entered. By this extravagant act, she said, "Jesus, I love you, and I want to serve you all of my days."

Keeping the image of Mary and her extravagant love in mind, ask the Holy Spirit to give you a deeper sense of worship. Meditate on all the blessings God has given you.

Ponder his incomparable work of redemption. Look back at the times God has rescued you at different times in your life. Lay aside any anxieties about the future or bitter regrets about the past.

Jesus loves you. He redeemed you. Let these truths penetrate your heart, so that praise and thanksgiving may well up in you. Your humble, grateful prayer is like sweet-smelling incense to him!

"Lord, how can I ever thank you for redeeming me and giving me new life?"

August 12

Be perfect, just as your heavenly Father is perfect.
(Matthew 5:48)

Scripture scholars point out that the Greek word translated as "perfect" in Matthew 5:48 indicates a process of becoming whole and complete. From this perspective, we can imagine Jesus saying, "Keep moving forward! Keep working on becoming the person I created you to be. Don't settle for anything less than the holiness of wholeness!"

How do we grow into this perfection?

It comes as we use our talents and gifts to glorify the Lord and lift up the people around us. It comes as we focus on removing roadblocks that God reveals in our life: perhaps an unresolved resentment, an unhealthy habit, or a skewed way of thinking.

Ask the Lord how he wants you to grow and change. Let him shine the light of his love on your heart. Let him show you things you can do to help bridge the gap between who you are and who you're meant to be.

"Lord Jesus, I believe that you are leading me to wholeness and holiness."

August 13

Your life is hidden with Christ in God. (Colossians 3:3)

We are baptized into Christ's death and resurrection. Like seeds, we are planted, "hidden with Christ," waiting for the time when we can burst forth in a new and fruitful life.

How long must we wait before this new life comes forth?

The transformation is not magical. Paul tells us that we must "put to death" our old lives of self-centeredness and sin (Colossians 3:5), so that we can be clothed with Jesus' love, kindness, compassion, and humility.

Let us turn to Jesus in prayer and ask him to conform our hearts to his, our minds to his, and our characters to his. We can face everyday decisions in faith and trust, asking God to lead us and guide us.

The good news is that Jesus wants to transform us. He has blazed the path for us. Every day he reaches out to us and pours his love upon us.

"Praise to you, Jesus, for putting my old life to death on the cross. By your Spirit, help me receive your new life each day."

August 14

*I stood before you
to speak on their behalf. (Jeremiah 18:20)*

God called Jeremiah to remind the people of Jerusalem that they belonged to him alone. For his trouble, Jeremiah endured contempt. He lost family and friends and suffered attempts on his life.

Rather than indulging in self-pity or vengeful desires, Jeremiah entered into intimate conversation with God. He ranted; he complained; he asked for wisdom and strength.

Jeremiah urged the people of Judah to be just as honest with God—and just as obedient. This kind of relationship could sustain them in difficulties.

God wants this same kind of intimate conversation with us. He wants us to tell him everything. Share with him your ups and downs, your victories and your defeats, your praise and your doubts, your gratitude and your complaints.

God also wants us to be willing to hear everything he has to say to us. Are we open to his responses?

Your Father cares about every detail of your life. Even now he is waiting to talk with you about everything.

"Father, I want to talk to you as Jeremiah did. Let me hear your voice and experience your presence today."

August 15

The kingdom of heaven is like a net thrown into the sea.
(Matthew 13:47)

Scripture is filled with stories of Jesus "fishing" for people: he rescued the woman caught in adultery, he had dinner with the tax collector Zacchaeus, he patiently taught the upright Pharisee Nicodemus. No matter where he went, Jesus cast his net, speaking and acting on the love of the Father and gathering people into his kingdom.

Jesus commanded his followers to also be "fishers of men" (Mark 1:17). And he calls us to the same task. Just as indiscriminately as Jesus did, God wants us to share the good news as often as we can. The catch can be huge!

You can tell people about the love of God, even by offering a smile and a kind greeting. You can pray the Lord's Prayer with your family. You can listen to a neighbor more than talking to them. And if the moment arises, you can tell any of these people, "God loves you."

Our care for people is attractive and infectious. So keep casting your nets!

"Holy Spirit, fill me with the desire to share the gospel. Use me to bring your love to everyone I meet."

August 16

Take courage, it is I, do not be afraid! (Mark 6:50)

Jesus sent his disciples out in a boat and headed for the hills to spend time alone with his Father. As he was praying, he could see his disciples struggling against the wind. So he interrupted his prayer, came to them on the water, and calmed the storm.

Are you rowing against the wind? What are you struggling with? Bring it before the Lord now.

Maybe he will reveal himself to you more deeply. He may even climb into your boat and still the wind. Perhaps in his wisdom the Lord will wait to respond, keeping his eyes on you till a more opportune moment.

Whatever happens, trust in Jesus' power and provision. Quiet your heart so that you can hear him tell you, "It is I, do not be afraid." Let him meet your needs in the way he knows best.

"Lord Jesus, help me find my courage in you. Right now I set aside fear and doubt. Lord, I trust you."

August 17

I am the bread of life; whoever comes to me will never hunger, and whoever believes in me will never thirst.
(John 6:35)

The crowd listening to Jesus couldn't figure him out. He was a prophet, no doubt, but he said and did things that stretched beyond their laws and traditions. He did things that only God could do, like heal the sick and forgive sins.

Peter was tenacious in following Jesus, despite baffling questions and answers. "Master," he asked, "to whom shall we go?" (John 6:68). No one else spoke with the authority, passion, and love of Jesus.

Sometimes we want to know exactly what God has for our lives. Should I stay at this job? Should I marry this person? Why wasn't my loved one healed? Sometimes he gives us a response, and other times we must wait. Whatever happens, let us stick with Jesus. He has "the words of eternal life" (John 6:68). He is our Lord!

"Lord, I believe that you are my 'bread of life.' Help me hold fast to you."

August 18

I am the vine, you are the branches. (John 15:5)

What a perfect image for our relationship with Jesus! It tells us that Jesus wants to suffuse us with life—his life, one that looks very different from the life we experience when we are not being nourished by the Lord.

So just what is it that Jesus gives us that we can't get on our own? It's not that we haven't been endowed with natural gifts of creativity, curiosity, or intelligence. Through education and perseverance, we can develop these gifts and accomplish many good things.

But being connected with Jesus, being nourished by him, fills these gifts and talents with new meaning, excitement, and purpose. It also means that we have divine life within us— and that involves even greater, spiritual gifts.

For example, as we stay connected to the Lord, we will find that our relationships are even more fulfilling. We will find divine strength to help us get through a difficult situation. We will find a joy that comes from deep within us, no matter what our circumstances. And above all of this, we will find a peace "that surpasses all understanding" (Philippians 4:7).

"Lord, you are the vine, and I am your branch. May I never forget how much I need you!"

August 19

Do not let your hearts be troubled. (John 14:27)

The disciples had more than enough reason to be troubled. Jesus was about to leave, but the "ruler of the world"— the Holy Spirit—was on his way (John 14:30). Jesus knew that his departure would bring them peace. From the Father's right hand, he would pour his Spirit into their hearts, and the Spirit would reveal God's love to them in new and deeper ways. Their anxious hearts would find rest.

How can we come to know God's love in this way?

How can we experience the peace that Jesus promised his disciples?

The key lies in dynamic prayer, asking the Holy Spirit to lift up our natural imagination and give us spiritual insight.

Imagine yourself with Jesus as he is about to be arrested and suffer death. Imagine Jesus talking right to you.

What message does he have for you today, and how can you best respond to him?

Let Jesus calm your anxious heart, just as he did for the disciples!

"Father, I want to know you more. Show me your majesty, your love, and your joy."

August 20

Give glory to your son, so that your son may glorify you.
(John 17:1)

In everything he did, Jesus sought to be the perfect reflection of his Father's glory. There is a lesson for us here.

Our true glory isn't in what we accomplish or how much recognition we receive. It's in the great privilege of knowing the Lord, being loved by him, and having him make his home in our hearts. Our glory is in God, just as it was for Jesus.

What will that look like for you today?

You probably have some routine tasks to perform—things that you've done countless times and for which you receive little recognition. Maybe it's making breakfast for the kids or making sure the bills get paid.

As you do these jobs, ask Jesus to be with you. Let them become acts of love for your family and worship for him.

Even if you seem invisible to the people around you, Jesus always sees you. You can glorify him by your love and faithfulness.

"Lord, help me find your peace, your joy, and your love in all that I do. Let me bring glory to your name!"

August 21

They recognized them as the companions of Jesus.
(Acts 4:13)

Peter and John were preaching the gospel with boldness. They healed a man who had been unable to walk for thirty-eight years, and everyone who witnessed the miracle was praising God. It was a scene of great excitement. But the thing that caught the attention of the elders and scribes was that these two men were companions of Jesus.

How does one recognize a companion?

After spending time with someone, you begin to share mannerisms and phrases. You share the person's ups and downs, griefs and joys. Companionship is not so much about *what you do* as it is about *who you become*.

Companionship with Jesus is even more than a close friendship. As we spend time with him, we become more like him. And that can only be good!

Invite Jesus to be with you as you go about your day. Talk to him in your heart. Share your experiences with him. And listen for his responses. Jesus wants to share his life with you. He wants to be your companion!

"Lord, I want to be your companion; help me walk through every day with you."

August 22

I have told you this so that my joy may be in you and your joy may be complete. (John 15:11)

Lots of people would pay a fortune for the secret to total joy. Jesus gives it for free!

You will have joy that is "complete," Jesus tells us, if you "remain in my love" (John 15:9).

And how do we do that?

"Keep my commandments . . . just as I have kept my Father's commandments" (John 15:9-10). God made us to be happy by abiding in him. "I delight to do your will" (Psalm 40:9).

Obedience is the golden key that unlocks room after room of spiritual treasures. Though sometimes painful and costly, obedience opens the way to the deepest longing of the human heart—to be with Jesus.

What does obedience mean for you?

Does your key to joy need a little dusting off?

"Jesus, help me walk through this day with the key of obedience in my hand. Show me the delights of obeying your will. Lead me into the joy of abiding in your love."

August 23

It is better for you that I go. (John 16:7)

The disciples couldn't imagine anything better than Jesus' company, teaching, healing, and declaring the good news of the kingdom. But Jesus knew his departure was better than his presence. He insisted, "It is better for you that I go" (John 16:7).

Why? Because having returned to the Father, he would send the Spirit: the Holy Spirit, the Spirit of God, to dwell in their hearts.

Yes, it would be exciting to watch Jesus perform awesome miracles. But there's a difference between being excited and being changed. Only by speaking deeply to our consciences can the Spirit move us. Only by taking Jesus' words and writing them on our hearts can the Spirit fill us with consolation, peace, and joy. Only by pouring God's love into us can the Spirit soften our hearts and move us to treat each other with mercy and compassion.

So the next time you find yourself thinking about how powerful it was when Jesus walked the earth, remind yourself that you already have the best thing. You have almighty God living in you.

"Jesus, thank you for sending the Holy Spirit. Open my ears to hear his voice and my heart to follow his leading."

August 24

Be like servants who await their master's return . . . , ready
to open immediately when he comes and knocks.
(Luke 12:36)

A re you ready? The servants in Jesus' story gird their loins,
light their lamps, and listen for their master's knock.
They keep dinner warm, and they're ready to hang up the
master's cloak and wash his feet when he arrives. They are
all set to serve their master.

The master commends them for being ready. Then comes
the surprise. He tells them to sit down at the table. "Tonight
I'm going to wait on you!"

So how will the Master surprise you today?

Yes, do all you can to carry out your responsibilities: make
sure you are obeying God's commands and loving other people as he has loved you. But also hold your heart in readiness.
God is full of surprises! He may give you an unexpected
token of his love.

"Lord Jesus, I want to be ready to welcome you whenever
you choose to knock on my door today."

August 25

They tried to go on into Bithynia, but the Spirit of Jesus did not allow them. (Acts 16:7)

We don't know what caused Paul to rethink his travel plans. The Holy Spirit often speaks to us through everyday situations. Maybe Paul found a road washed out by an unexpected flood. A severe storm may have prevented travel to a certain area. Or perhaps a traveling companion was taken ill, and they had to make a detour for medical help.

Instead of trying to force his original plan, Paul accepted the change with grace and confidence that the Holy Spirit would guide him.

Sometimes discernment is a process by which we hear the Holy Spirit speaking to us clearly. At other times, changing circumstances or detours may be the "voice" God uses to help us reformulate our plans. We should always be open to the ways God may lead us.

As we embrace new itineraries that come from the Lord, we will find blessing and fruitfulness!

"Holy Spirit, teach me to recognize the ways you speak to me. Open my ears to your direction in the ordinary events of my day."

August 26

[He] is able to accomplish far more than all we ask or imagine, by the power at work within us. (Ephesians 3:20)

Whether you recognize it or not, you are an important player in the unfolding of God's master plan. Your words, your actions, your demeanor are helping shape other people and their perception of the Lord. Even your prayers are changing the world!

How can we advance God's plan when we are dealing with our own mistakes and weaknesses?

Paul's prayer for the Ephesians urges us not to worry. There is a mighty power at work within us! Our job is to try our best to connect with the Holy Spirit every day.

God needs someone in your corner of the world at this time in history. He knows what you can do. Even in your imperfections, you are the perfect fit for the work God has for you.

So let yourself become God's instrument. Cooperate with his Spirit, and you'll change the world.

"Lord, help me remember that you are at work in me and through me. Help me surrender to you and rejoice in you."

August 27

*A woman was there who for eighteen years
had been crippled by a spirit. (Luke 13:11)*

Imagine how this woman's affliction affected her life. Jewish thinking at the time made a correlation between illness and sin (see John 9:2). People probably avoided her, not only because of her crippled appearance but because of her apparent sin.

Perhaps the woman searched her heart for what she had done to deserve this burden. At the same time, she persevered in her faith in God. Why else would she have been at the synagogue?

Jesus spoke words of freedom to her, and he touched her. Suddenly she was able to stand. Not only did Jesus straighten her back; he freed her from guilt and isolation. Her reaction was to praise God!

Many things can keep us from standing up and giving glory to God: an illness, a fractured relationship, a past sin. Is it too hard for Jesus to handle? Absolutely not!

Follow this woman's lead. Go to Jesus, in the "synagogue" of your heart. Ask him to see you, touch you, and set you free.

"Father, you have created me to live in freedom. Release me from everything that burdens my spirit."

August 28

They shook the dust from their feet. (Acts 13:51)

Even the apostles encountered disappointments in their mission when they weren't welcomed in a community. Rather than give in to discouragement, they shook the dust from their feet, as Jesus had instructed (see Luke 9:5). They commended the people to God and moved on.

What would shaking the dust look like for you?

First, forgive. Don't let resentment weigh you down. Trust that God will take care of whatever situation you cannot resolve.

Second, let go. Leave the situation in God's hands, so you are free to take the next good step.

Third, move on. Maybe God wants to show you a different path. Maybe you need some time away from the situation to regroup and let the Lord step in.

Forgive, let go, move on—always in a spirit of patience and love. Keep praying, and trust that the Lord will work out his plan according to his wisdom in his own time.

"Lord, help me shake off any 'dust' of resentment, disappointment, and frustration. Jesus, I trust in your timing."

August 29

Let us love . . . in deed and truth. (1 John 3:18)

John offers us solid guidance on how to remain in God's love. One of the secrets is to listen to the movements of our hearts; for the heart, or the conscience, is the place where the Holy Spirit speaks to us most intimately. As the prophet Jeremiah promised, God writes his word on our hearts (see 31:33).

The Holy Spirit helps us, giving us "confidence in God" (1 John 3:21) as we follow his commands and letting our hearts "condemn" us when we act selfishly (3:20).

We should take seriously any tug in our heart. Movements there may well indicate that the Spirit is leading us. He forms our hearts and helps us make good decisions. He's even at work when we aren't aware of him!

Remain in God's love today. Listen to the movements of your heart, and try to put into practice whatever you think God is asking of you.

"Holy Spirit, come and move in my life. Inspire me to do good deeds in spirit and in truth."

August 30

You did not recognize the time of your visitation.
(Luke 19:44)

God often comes to us in subtle ways. He might visit you in a gentle conviction of sin that moves you to repent. He might come in an inspiration to do something you've never considered. Maybe he will whisper a thought that persists over the course of days and weeks. Or he might give you a quiet assurance in wakeful hours of the night.

Often God "visits" us through Scripture. Maybe a passage swells your heart with hope, or one word stands out, as if the Lord has underlined it just for you.

Recognize these visits from God. Pause and think about what emotions God is stirring in you and what thoughts come to mind. What might God want to say to you?

Jesus came in the flesh to show us how deeply he wants to be united with us. He placed his Holy Spirit in us so that we could recognize his coming.

"Father, thank you for revealing your presence to me. Lead me in your truth, and guide me today and always."

August 31

I was only pouring out my heart to the Lord.
(1 Samuel 1:15)

Hannah poured out her heart to the Lord. Tears streamed down her face as she silently begged the Lord for a child. God heard her prayer. Hannah became pregnant not long after this and bore a son, Samuel.

When was the last time you poured out your heart to the Lord?

Are you reluctant to tell him your woes?

Perhaps you feel that you're supposed to accept everything with a stiff upper lip or that it's presumptuous to ask God for things.

Hannah is a model for us. Tell the Lord what is on your mind—even if you are upset with him about your situation. Tell him how you feel. And be sure to listen carefully to what God says to you. You can't predict how he will answer you, but you can be certain that you will experience his healing and grow in hope and confidence. You will grow closer to him.

"Lord, you know all my deepest desires and fears. I turn to you today, trusting that you will hear my prayer and answer me."

Notes

_____

_____

_____

_____

_____

_____

_____

_____

_____

_____

_____

_____

_____

_____

_____

_____

September

JESUS UNITES
ME TO HIS BODY

September 1

Wherever you go I will go. (Ruth 1:16)

We learn in Scripture that God is eager to protect the stranger, the orphan, and the widow.

How does he do this?

He uses people, often people who are struggling themselves or who have experienced past trials. And who better to help someone in need than someone who knows what it's like to be alone or downtrodden?

If you read the story of Ruth you would find that we don't have to be perfect before we can minister God's love. We simply have to be willing to offer ourselves. We may feel inadequate because of our own challenges, but that may be just as God wants it. After all, the word "compassion" means "to suffer with."

When we give ourselves to help another person, something wonderful happens. By picking up that person's cross, we meet Jesus in a powerful way—just as Simon of Cyrene did on the way to Calvary.

Jesus' whole life was one of service. As he was raised to the Father's right hand because he emptied himself, we can be too.

Whose cross can you help carry?

"Lord, help me bring your love to the people around me."

September 2

*I thought that he would surely come out to me and stand
there to call on the name of the LORD his God.*
(2 Kings 5:11)

Naaman carefully planned his journey in search of healing,
but he kept having to adjust his expectations. Offended
by what Elisha told him to do, Naaman was ready to go home
without being healed. His servants persuaded him that he
might as well try. Not only was Naaman healed; he came to
know the one true God.

Do our notions of how things should be blind us to what
God wants to do for us?

Fortunately, God has agents, like Naaman's servants, who
can help correct our course. It may be a character from Scripture or a present-day hero whose triumph speaks to our lives.
It may be a wise friend who prays with us or simply listens
and asks questions that help us get unstuck.

If you face a challenge or an important decision, lay it
before the Lord, and ask him to direct you. Then open your
eyes and ears! He has his agents in strategic locations, ready
to move you along his path.

"Lord, send your messengers to shine light on my path."

September 3

You are . . . members of the household of God.
(Ephesians 2:19)

Of all the special places in our lives—our hometown, our school sports team, a political party—none compare to the loyalty we feel toward our family and close friends. So when Paul tells us that we have become "members of the household of God," part of God's own family, it means a lot!

Committing our highest loyalties to Jesus helps us in all our other commitments. We find new wisdom for raising our children and loving our spouse. The Holy Spirit empowers us to make a good contribution at work, even as our peace witnesses to the joy of the gospel. Human logic and reason can offer us insights in these areas, but how much more we can receive when we are connected to the Lord!

Jesus wants our identity as members of his household to loom larger than anything else, so that it can guide everything we do and say. He wants to be our shepherd and our friend as we surrender to him.

"Lord, thank you for bringing me into your family."

September 4

The gates of the netherworld shall not prevail.
(Matthew 16:18)

Each of us probably knows someone who is struggling with their faith or who has left it behind. Yet Jesus promised that the gates of hell would never prevail against his followers. How can we believe this?

Perhaps the best place to start is by taking these words personally.

What role do we play in fulfilling Jesus' promise that the devil won't win?

The answer is to stay close to Jesus. He has won the battle against the devil. The powers of darkness cannot sway us if we stay connected to the Lord. In him we will find the strength to stand firm.

Be faithful to daily prayer. Read and study Scripture. Serve Jesus in the poor and needy. As you do, you push back the devil and his power. You strengthen and defend all your brothers and sisters around the world.

Be confident in Jesus' promise. He is victorious in his body of believers!

"Jesus, you give life to each of your followers. Strengthen your body on earth."

September 5

What did you go out to the desert to see? (Luke 7:24)

Jesus confronted the religious leaders who were speaking ill of John the Baptist because of his asceticism. These same leaders grumbled that Jesus spent time with tax collectors and sinners. It seems that they condemned anything that fell outside of their boundaries. Their expectations left no room for the freedom of the Holy Spirit.

This might lead us to consider: how rigid am I?

We can answer by examining our spiritual lives:

Do I enjoy the freedom to live as Jesus is leading me?

Am I free to respond to his Spirit in the way I sense he is calling me?

Some people are called to contemplation, others to exuberance. Some are called to serve the poor, others to work for social change. The important point for each of us is to love Jesus, keep his commands, and build the kingdom of God.

Let's try our best to love and serve God. Let's also respect what he calls others to do.

"Father, I rejoice in the freedom I have as your child. I trust you and will follow you wherever you lead!"

September 6

You are my friends. (John 15:14)

A good friend is a great joy and blessing, and Jesus proved himself the best of friends. His compassion was like a magnet drawing people to him. Outcasts like the adulterous woman in Luke 7, the cheating tax collector in Luke 19, and the "good thief" in Luke 23 all approached him with confidence.

Jesus knew that his disciples would abandon and betray him, and yet he called them his friends (see John 15:15). He declared to them the true mark of friendship: he would lay down his life for them (see 15:13).

Jesus calls each of us his friend, and he invites us to join him in laying down our lives for the poor, the needy, and the neglected. They are all around us: in our church, in our neighborhood, in the stores where we shop, on the streets that we travel.

Are our eyes open to see them?

Let us make room in our lives for the people around us. We will find ourselves touching not just a lonely person but Jesus himself!

"Lord, teach me how to be a true friend to the people around me."

September 7

Blessed are you who believed. (Luke 1:45)

Mary was joyful about the news that God had chosen her to bear his Son. Learning that her cousin Elizabeth was also expecting, Mary "set out and traveled to the hill country in haste" (Luke 1:39). Together she and Elizabeth celebrated the great things God was doing.

How important it is that we support one another! The right words from a trusted companion can strengthen us for the work to which God calls us. We can help each other simply by our presence. Attentive listening and words of encouragement also give energy, enthusiasm, and hope in our service for the kingdom.

Let us value the brotherhood and sisterhood that God has given us. He calls husbands and wives to see the treasure that they are to each other, parents to enjoy their children, neighbors to reach out, and all to support the poor.

Every day God gives us opportunities to meet Jesus in each other. Let's together allow our hearts to leap for joy.

"Jesus, you are the light that shines in the darkness. Make me into that light, shining for others who need your support and love."

September 8

Elijah will indeed come. (Matthew 17:11)

God sent an Elijah in the time of Jesus: John the Baptist prepared the way by preaching repentance. He baptized the people who came to him, and many of them turned back to God. Some became Jesus' first disciples.

God sent an Elijah in your life, someone whose example had an impact on you. You wanted to have faith like they had. You wanted to know the Scriptures as well as they did. You wanted their peace and joy. So you spent time with them and listened to what they had to say. They were your Elijah! Their influence opened your eyes and softened your heart to receive the Lord more deeply.

Do you know someone who needs an Elijah in their life?

God will send an Elijah into the lives of your loved ones. You can pray with confidence for God to send someone to the person you are most concerned about: your child or grandchild, brother or sister, neighbor or coworker. God wants his life to grow in each one of them.

Be encouraged. Elijah will come!

"Heavenly Father, you want each person to receive your Son! I trust you to send someone to prepare the way!"

September 9

Here I am, Lord. (Acts 9:10)

God asked Ananias to do something downright dangerous: approach a man named Saul who was hunting down Christians and putting them to death. Ananias courageously did as God asked.

Surely God could have healed Saul on his own. But God knew how valuable human connection can be. Saul needed to experience kindness from a believer as strong as Ananias, as a way to soften his heart. Ananias would also testify to the authenticity of Saul's conversion, assuring other believers that Saul was on their side.

God might ask us to bring healing to people in need, even some who do not like us. Of course, we pray for them, but sometimes God wants us to offer healing hands as well. He wants us to embody his mercy, his love, and his healing for the many people who need a gentle touch, a warm smile, and words of compassion.

Are we ready and courageous enough to say, "Here I am, Lord!" and step forward in faith?

"Lord, give me the wisdom, courage, and faith to reach out to the people around me who need to know your healing touch."

September 10

Lavishly he gives to the poor. (Psalm 112:9)

The word "lavish" has its roots in the Latin word *lavare*, which means "to wash." Psalm 112 tells us that the righteous person literally showers the poor with what they need.

In one sense, we are all poor. We are wounded by sin, and we live in a fallen world. Jesus is lavish toward us, showering us with mercy, wisdom through the Scriptures, the guidance and insights of the Holy Spirit. So much refreshment, so many riches!

All these lavish gifts aren't meant just for us. God wants us to be generous as well.

What else can we do with such abundance?

We don't have room to keep it all to ourselves! Everyone who has tasted of God's goodness can't help but share it with others.

Let the word "lavish" remind you of Jesus' generosity toward you. And let it remind you to be generous with the people around you.

"Thank you, Lord, for showering me with your grace. Give me a generous heart."

September 11

Go to my own land and to my relatives to get a wife for my son Isaac. (Genesis 24:4)

Abraham and Sarah had received the promise from God; now it was Isaac's turn. He had to find a woman willing to leave her home and embrace God's call. Isaac's choice was Rebekah, who took her place in the line of matriarchs who joined their husbands in honoring God and dedicating themselves to his purposes. She helped her husband stay faithful to God. She taught her children about the covenant they were called to embrace.

How wonderful it is when a husband and wife work together toward a common goal!

St. Paul teaches that the love between a husband and wife can manifest Jesus' love for his church (see Ephesians 5:23-33).

If you are married, take time to celebrate your life together. Thank the Lord for the gift that your spouse is to you.

And if you are single, pray for marriages everywhere. May the Lord pour extra grace on all married couples!

"Father, strengthen every husband and wife in unity, so they can manifest your covenant love to the world!"

September 12

See that you do not despise one of these little ones.
(Matthew 18:10)

The disciples were surprised when Jesus used a little child to answer their question "Who is the greatest in the kingdom of heaven?" (Matthew 18:1). He didn't choose a scholar, a ruler, or a wealthy man; he chose a little one no one else would call great.

If we want to draw near to God, we'll find him when we stoop down and put our arms around a little one. We'll get to know him by going to the fringes in search of the lost and the lonely.

We tend to make allowances for little children. Preschoolers who don't know which way to run on the soccer field are adorable. Noises that would be obnoxious coming from a teenager sound cute on the lips of a four-year-old.

God the Father regards us as his children, his "little ones" to be honored and loved. We don't need to impress him in order to earn his favor. He seizes on the slightest kernel of goodness in everything we do and encourages us to develop it.

"Jesus, sometimes I get confused about what really matters. Help me value each individual as much as you do."

September 13

[John] was a burning and shining lamp. (John 5:35)

In April 1917, a young Edith Stein, an agnostic, went to visit Anna Reinach, a friend whose husband had just died in battle. Edith found Anna—though deeply grieving—surprisingly radiant with hope in the resurrection. That meeting was "the moment when my unbelief collapsed and Christ began to shine his light on me—Christ in the mystery of the cross." Anna was like John the Baptist, "a burning and shining lamp" bearing witness to the light of Christ.

The light of Christ continues to shine through his disciples. It even shines in you! Every time you bite your tongue instead of retaliating, his light shines. Every time you reach out to a hurting neighbor, his light shines. Every time you take time to pray, his light shines.

Wouldn't it be wonderful if each day we would all do one small thing that let the light of Christ shine?

We are the light of the world. Even lamps that are nicked or battered can shine. So let your light shine!

"Lord, help me welcome your light into every corner of my life. May I shine so that the people around me might glorify you."

September 14

They came bringing to him a paralytic. . . . When Jesus saw their faith, he said to the paralytic, "Child, your sins are forgiven." (Mark 2:3, 5)

Jesus forgave this man and then healed his paralysis because he saw the faith of his friends. These four men loved their friend enough—and believed in Jesus enough—to tear up the roof to get the man to Jesus!

Jesus never intended the Christian life to be a solitary journey. On the contrary, we are stronger when we are surrounded and supported by brothers and sisters in the faith. Jesus tells us to lean on each other—and to let others lean on us. He sent his disciples to preach "two by two" (Mark 6:7). He knew they needed the help of one another in moments of weakness and in the face of opposition or hardship.

What about you? Do you have brothers and sisters to help bring you to Jesus?

Never doubt that God wants to give you companions along the way. And you can be such a companion to someone else. Your faith can make all the difference in another person's life.

May we all be open to the generous gift of one another.

"Lord, you promised that you would be with us always. Thank you for fulfilling that promise through faithful friends!"

September 15

Here are my mother and my brothers. (Matthew 12:49)

Every human being has a deep desire to belong, to be part of a loving family, to be respected, to be understood, to be loved. If you identify with these longings, could it be what you are saying deep down is "I want to belong to God and his family"?

Jesus says that "whoever does the will of my heavenly Father is my brother, and sister, and mother" (Matthew 12:50). Something more powerful than a bloodline defines who belongs to his family.

Surely Jesus knew what an immature, motley crew his followers were. We read, "The word remained hidden from them and they failed to comprehend what he said" (Luke 18:34). What Jesus saw in them was more a potential than a reality.

Jesus placed this band of disciples on par with his own mother, and he thinks the same about you. You try to please him, to follow him, to become more like him. Of course you're going to stumble along the way. But you can be sure of this reality: Jesus loves you just as you are right now.

"Jesus, thank you for making me part of your forever family."

September 16

You shall love your neighbor as yourself. (Leviticus 19:18)

How can we observe what Jesus calls the "two great commandments" of the Law: "You shall love the Lord, your God, with all your heart" and "You shall love your neighbor as yourself" (Matthew 22:37, 39)?

In Leviticus there are plenty of specifics about loving your neighbor: Don't steal or cheat. Don't take advantage of the poor. Don't disparage those with disabilities. Don't stand by idly when someone is in need. Jesus is just as specific. He calls us to look into the eyes of someone who is poor, hungry, homeless, sick, or imprisoned, and treat him or her as we would treat the Lord.

Jesus tells us, "These are all 'least brothers of mine' (Matthew 25:40). When you look at them, you see me. When you serve them, you serve me. When you love them, you are loving me."

Do we see opportunities to meet Jesus in the people around us? Let us strive to love one another, and we will love Jesus!

"Jesus, open my eyes, so that I can see you and love you in my neighbor."

September 17

I give you a new commandment. . . . As I have loved you, so you also should love one another. (John 13:34)

The second great commandment, Jesus said, is to love our neighbor as we love ourselves (see Matthew 22:39). He took this further as he spoke to his disciples on the night before he died. He wants us to love one another as he loves us. This is what will set us apart as his people, his bride.

If you want to know what Jesus' love looks like, think about Scripture passages that have touched your heart and about your personal experiences of the Lord.

Is his love generous? forgiving? compassionate? Is it faithful? trustworthy? pure? Take one of the descriptions on your list and focus on living it out today.

Thank Jesus for the way he loves you, and ask him to put that same love in your heart. This is what will set you apart as a member of the bride of Christ.

"Come, Lord, and expand my love. I want to be your bride in this world!"

September 18

What I do have I give you: in the name of Jesus Christ the Nazorean, [rise and] walk. (Acts 3:6)

Every day as they went to the Temple, Peter and John walked past a lame beggar. He must have seemed insignificant compared to his surroundings, for they never really took note of him.

But one day the Holy Spirit opened Peter's and John's eyes. They saw how precious and beautiful the man was. They confidently invited him to be healed. And God healed him!

The beauty of the world is always before us, and we should appreciate it. God also wants to open our eyes to its veiled treasures. He wants us to look more closely at the people we pass every day and see how precious they are to him.

Imagine that we can bring healing, restoration, and peace to this world as we see the beauty and glory in every person!

"Lord, help me see how precious people are in your eyes. Fill me with your love and compassion. Give me the courage to extend your love to them."

September 19

The church . . . was being built up and walked
in the fear of the Lord. (Acts 9:31)

The believers in the early church felt connected to one
another. Paul "traveled in orderly sequence . . . , bringing strength to all the disciples" (Acts 18:23). Priscilla and
Aquila instructed the newly converted Apollos, and he became
an important part of their mission to spread the good news
(see 18:24-28).

Though the church has changed in many ways over the centuries, we still need one another. Maybe we can help someone
understand their faith better. That person may in turn share
Christ with others—just as Apollos did! Or perhaps we can
encourage a friend or our spouse to develop a daily prayer
time—and then give him or her the time and space to do so, or
offer to watch a friend's children while they attend a retreat.

The church flourishes when its members are committed
to one another. We all benefit when we turn to one another
for strength, encouragement, wisdom, and love.

How might you help?

"Lord, help me see how much I need my brothers and sisters
and how much they need me. Give me a generous heart to
meet those needs."

September 20

They sent Barnabas [to go] to Antioch. . . . He was a good man, filled with the holy Spirit and faith. (Acts 11:22, 24)

Jesus' followers knew that when zealous, excited people get together, they need a guiding hand and some skilled mediation. So when a new church sprang up in Antioch, consisting of both Jews and Gentiles, the apostles sent Barnabas.

This man's real name was Joseph, but the apostles nicknamed him Barnabas, which means "son of encouragement" (Acts 4:36). Every time Barnabas appears in Acts or Paul's letters, it is as a peacemaker, as someone widely respected.

How can we bring peace to a stressful situation so that people come together in harmony?

A great clue is in Barnabas's name: *encouragement*. The first step in peacemaking can be a simple boost: "You're doing great!" Genuinely encouraging words can soften hearts and bring reconciliation.

Barnabas, on arriving in Antioch, "saw the grace of God, . . . rejoiced and encouraged them all to remain faithful to the Lord in firmness of heart" (Acts 11:23).

Let's take a cue from this apostle and become sons and daughters of encouragement!

"Lord, help me be a peacemaker and serve you faithfully."

September 21

Jesus didn't seem to be taking care of himself. We know from other passages that he often cut short his sleep to spend hours in prayer. He gave up his trade to become a wandering preacher. And he cut himself off from the most important of social ties—his home and family.

Many of us know people who pour themselves out for God: missionaries in foreign lands, people who care for elderly relatives, single parents, pastors, and more. Each is a reflection of the way Jesus constantly poured himself out.

It's never a waste to pour yourself out for the Lord and his people, to spend the night in prayer or to forgo some comfort in the name of love. God sees the sacrifices we make, and he blesses them.

Let's pray for God's zealous servants. And if you feel pushed to your limits by the call to love, ask your brothers and sisters in Christ to stand with you in prayer.

"Lord Jesus, thank you for the sacrifices your servants make in your name. Come, Lord, and sustain them in your love."

September 22

Remember your leaders who spoke the word of God to you. . . . and imitate their faith. (Hebrews 13:7)

You most likely have people in your life who encouraged you in your walk of faith. So how can you honor them?

First, the Letter to the Hebrews tells us, remember who they are. Maybe your parents encouraged you in their day-to-day life with you. Maybe a neighbor enlarged your faith, or a friend helped you trust the Lord more deeply. If possible, find a way to thank these people. And of course, pray for them.

Next, Hebrews tells us, imitate their faith. Perhaps someone's prayer life has inspired you; try to follow his or her example. If you were touched by someone's humble way of caring for people, try to reach out in that way to someone else.

You'll likely find that imitating others' faith will make you an inspiration to someone. That's the way faith works: we all influence each other. And so the kingdom of God continues to grow.

"Lord, thank you for the people who have helped me grow closer to you. Help me imitate their faith and be a witness to others."

September 23

*Whoever is angry with his brother will
be liable to judgment. (Matthew 5:22)*

Let's face it. It's hard not to get angry—even with those
who are closest to us!

Jesus calls us to turn away from anger. As difficult as that
sounds, it does make sense. Our eternal destiny is heaven,
where we will live in peace and unity with each other and
Almighty God. But we don't have to wait until the Second
Coming for unity to prevail.

The heart of the gospel message is that Jesus died to forgive our sins so that we could be transformed. In fact, he
knows that we can keep his law of love only as we keep our
eyes focused on him in prayer.

God puts his own Holy Spirit in us to enable us to fulfill
his commands—even those that seem impossible. We have
the grace to resist temptation. Every time we find anger pull-
ing us in the wrong direction, we can pray, "Jesus, I believe
in your grace. I ask for your help right now."

We can win the spiritual battle by combining our efforts
with trust in God's power. Together we really can become holy!

*"Lord Jesus, thank you for your marvelous grace! Help me
love as you do."*

September 24

The word of the Lord was rare in those days.
(1 Samuel 3:1, NRSV)

Think of how God communicates with his people. In the Old Testament, God usually spoke through his prophets. When Jesus poured out his Spirit on Pentecost, the apostles received power to spread the good news throughout the known world in a very short time. We have inherited their mission—and what a revolutionary mission it is!

We carry the news that death has been vanquished and that there's no reason to fear. It's not just the next life but this life that can be transformed through the power of Christ.

The call to evangelize may seem intimidating, but you aren't responsible for converting someone else—just for giving what you have.

Think about one person you know who needs Jesus. Pray about how you can witness God's love to that person. Take a step of faith, and see how far the Spirit will carry it.

You can become proof that revelation of the Lord is no longer uncommon!

"Lord, help me plant a seed of love in someone's life today."

September 25

Jesus himself drew near and walked with them, but their eyes were prevented from recognizing him.
(Luke 24:15-16)

Life can certainly be messy at times. Perhaps there are times when we feel unable to move forward, begging our way through each day, not knowing what tomorrow will bring.

Cleopas and his companion were heartbroken. The man they thought was the Messiah had been killed on a cross. They shared their disappointments with the stranger who walked beside them. They felt safe in pouring out their hearts to him. They were also open to his reply.

Just as Jesus walked with these disciples, we can trust that God is with us, even in the messy parts of our lives.

How do we find him? The reading suggests that we share our burdens and look for him in the people around us.

When you feel helpless, remember to see if God is sending you help. Part of the adventure of Christianity is that you never know whom the Lord will use!

We are not supposed to take up this Christian life all alone. St. Paul refers to the church as the body of Christ, and for a reason: we are brothers and sisters called to help one another.

"Lord, teach me how to find you in the people around me."

September 26

I urge . . . that you be united. (1 Corinthians 1:10)

At the Last Supper, Jesus prayed that his people would be united (see John 17:21). He also prayed that the mark of his disciples would be their love for one another (see 13:34-35). Paul pleads for this unity in the Corinthian church.

Imagine how attractive the Church would be if we made it our highest priority to love each other as brothers and sisters. Imagine how magnetic the Church would be if we looked upon each other as children of God trying to love God and serve him.

Unity means honoring and respecting everyone—including those with whom we disagree. It comes when we recognize that the dignity of all human persons is in the fact that we are created in the image and likeness of God (see Genesis 1:26-27).

Nothing is impossible with God. Let us take St. Paul's exhortation to be united and make it our own.

What will be the single most compelling thing that will move people to believe in Jesus? Our unity. Our love for each other.

"Come, Lord, and heal all divisions. Make our churches and families beacons of your love."

September 27

*Their profound poverty overflowed in a
wealth of generosity. (2 Corinthians 8:2)*

If someone is experiencing poverty, wouldn't you expect him
to rein in his spending and conserve his resources? If he is
hurt or suffering, wouldn't you expect him to rest, nurse his
wounds, and rebuild his strength?

Despite their poverty and suffering, the faith and joy of
the Macedonian Christians overflowed in generosity. They
even begged for the privilege of helping the church in Jerusalem. Paul gives a key for understanding this: "They gave
themselves first to the Lord" (2 Corinthians 8:5).

Jesus was their model: "For your sake he became poor
although he was rich, so that by his poverty you might become
rich" (2 Corinthians 8:9). More than that, Jesus' life within
them compelled them to respond.

The Macedonians believed that God would take care of
their needs if they gave priority to the needs of other members
of the body of Christ. We too can trust in our loving Father.

Remember, Jesus is our model, and he lives in us. Ask him
to help you see him in the faces of his needy children.

*"Father, I can never outdo you in generosity. Open my eyes
and my heart to the needs of all your children."*

September 28

Luke is the only one with me. (2 Timothy 4:11)

One of the most constant friendships in the early Church was the one between Luke and Paul. These friends shared their belief in Christ with each other—and with everyone they met.

Luke, a learned man, was an excellent listener. Imagine the time he spent listening to the "eyewitnesses from the beginning and ministers of the word," listening to their stories and to the Spirit as he wrote his Gospel and the Book of Acts (Luke 1:2).

Showing his true heart, Luke was with Paul in his missionary journeys, sharing hardships and challenges. And when Paul was imprisoned in Rome, Luke remained with him, offering encouragement and companionship (see 2 Timothy 4:11).

Today, think about your friends, especially those who have led you closer to Jesus. Think about friends who have been faithful to you through thick and thin. Thank and praise the Lord for them.

A faithful friend is a priceless treasure, a gift from God.

"Thank you, Lord, for the gift of my friends. Teach me to be as faithful to them as you have been to me."

September 29

They took him aside and explained to him the Way [of God] more accurately. (Acts 18:26)

Apollos knew Scripture and was an eloquent speaker. He also cared deeply about spreading the gospel. But his knowledge of the message was limited, so the seasoned Priscilla and Aquila took him aside and filled in the gaps.

How do you advise others? How often have you had to offer feedback—or even correction—to someone?

Priscilla and Aquila offer a good model to follow. They treated Apollos with respect and dignity. They quietly "took him aside," helped him see where his message was missing the mark, and steered him in a better direction.

As Paul wrote, we need to keep "a gentle spirit" about us (Galatians 6:1). We should be careful to build up, not tear down. We don't want to limit someone's willingness to use their God-given talents but rather help those talents flourish and bear fruit.

Your words may have a profound effect on someone. Just look at Apollos: he went on to give "great assistance" to new believers everywhere (Acts 18:27).

"Jesus, teach me how to give—and receive—feedback in a spirit of humility and gentleness."

September 30

*Everyone who loves the father loves [also]
the one begotten by him. (1 John 5:1)*

John observes that it's not possible to love God but not love the people he has created. The Father "shows up" in all his children. This is especially true of our brothers and sisters in the faith, since his Holy Spirit lives in their hearts.

So why can it be so hard to love other people sometimes? Perhaps it isn't easy to see the Father in his children. It might be easier to spot a person's faults. But John makes another observation: "The victory that conquers the world is our faith" (1 John 5:4).

Faith is the gift of being able to see what is hidden. Sometimes the Father's likeness in his children is just that—hidden. It calls for the eyes of faith to see that although someone may rub you the wrong way, that person is still worthy of your love and honor because God loves and honors him or her.

Is there someone you're having a difficult time loving right now? Imagine Jesus standing beside that person. See how much he loves them. Think about the special gifts God has equipped them with and the unique way they reflect his glory. Now do you see the resemblance?

"Father, help me see people with the eyes of faith. Show me how they reflect your beauty."

October

FRUIT THAT
WILL LAST

October 1

*He is like a tree
planted near streams of water,
that yields its fruit in season. (Psalm 1:3)*

Think about planting—not flowers and vegetables but yourself. Plant yourself near the river of life, the river that is "flowing from the throne of God" (Revelation 22:1). Send roots down deep into the rich soil of faith.

The best way to do this is to read and ponder the Scriptures each day. Don't just plow through the words, but stop to consider what they mean. Listen for the voice of the Spirit in your heart. Ask him how the words you read apply to your life. Don't go on until the Spirit has shone his light on them.

What will you hear? Maybe you'll hear Jesus saying: "Neither do I condemn you" as you ponder past sins or wonder if you'll ever break free of present ones (John 8:11). Or maybe you'll hear him say: "Come to me . . . and I will give you rest" (Matthew 11:28), and you will know for sure that he is with you in a hard situation.

The psalmist promises that whoever "meditates day and night" (Psalm 1:2) on God's word will bear fruit.

"Holy Spirit, help me settle myself near the river of life. I want to sink my roots deeply into the word of God, so that I can bear fruit in his kingdom."

October 2

Be fruitful and multiply, and fill the earth.
(Genesis 9:1, NRSV)

God issues Noah an invitation to participate in the ongoing creation of the world. We too have an important role in the unfolding of the kingdom of God. God invites us to make this world reflect the glory of the world to come!

Building the kingdom is no easy job. Every day we encounter terrible realities that are part of a fallen world: drug and alcohol abuse, domestic violence, unemployment, and the neglect of the elderly. We might need to dirty ourselves a bit as we serve God.

Even if we're not on the front lines, we all have a mission field. We are co-creators with God whenever we follow his commandment of love: nurturing our families to become his lights to the world; sharing the good news with our neighbors; and praying for the needs of others. Even seemingly insignificant actions can bring God's kingdom!

God doesn't send us out alone; his strength is with us. He has given us gifts and talents to bring about his vision for the world. Get in touch with your unique gifts and talents and put them to use.

"Fill our hearts, Lord, and send us out to transform this world for you."

October 3

Their leaves will not wither, nor will their fruit fail.
(Ezekiel 47:12)

In a vision, the prophet Ezekiel saw a stream of water flowing from the Temple. The water flowed to the Dead Sea in such abundance and vitality that it freshened that whole body of stagnant water. All along its banks, people were able to fish and obtain fresh water to sustain life.

This vision foreshadows the work of Christ. The Temple in Jerusalem was the place where God dwelled and where worship was centered. When Jesus became man, he became a new temple, opening the way to heaven, where all God's people live in lasting peace and fulfillment. Through his death on the cross, Jesus rescued us from exile and captivity to sin so that we could drink the life-giving water of his Holy Spirit.

What water are you drinking these days?

If we seek to quench our thirst through material possessions, sensual fulfillment, or esteem from others, we will never be satisfied.

We were created for God, and only he can give us the water that produces life, bringing healing and refreshment to us and to our world.

"Come, Holy Spirit, and fill me with your life. I want to bear fruit for the kingdom!"

October 4

The tottering gird on strength. (1 Samuel 2:4)

Hannah went from weeping to joyfully proclaiming God's faithfulness when God gave her a son. "That's easy for Hannah," we might think. "God answered her prayer." But Hannah changed before she conceived Samuel. Her despair lifted at a few words from Eli.

We all have times when our faith feels weak. God stands ready to strengthen us and steady us with his peace. All he asks is that we lean on him and let him fill us with his grace.

Like Hannah, we can persevere in seeking the Lord and his strength—even when we question whether anything will come of it. We can believe that his grace is girding us, even when we don't feel it.

Hannah was honest with God. We too can freely tell God how we feel. He won't be surprised or put off. He sees it all anyway!

God may not always grant our requests, but he will always give us his peace. And God's peace will give us the strength to trust him, even in our challenges.

So bring Jesus your concerns, your doubts, and your fears. Persevere, and be honest with him. Let him tell you what Eli told Hannah: "Go in peace" (1 Samuel 1:17).

"Jesus, I need your strength today. Come and fill me."

October 5

I shall cultivate the ground around it and fertilize it; it may bear fruit in the future. (Luke 13:8-9)

The parable of the fig tree tells us that God is constantly at work in us. He never gives up on us. He never condemns or rejects us. Our God always encourages us.

Jesus knows who we are. He knows everything about us. It's comforting to know that, even with our weaknesses and failures, Jesus will work in us to make us more fruitful. In fact, his compassion is one of the most effective fertilizers around. It's capable of feeding us and strengthening us. It has the power to lift us out of the pain and setbacks we experience and encourage us to take the next step forward to a fruitful, peaceful life.

If you ever find yourself feeling "troubled and abandoned, like sheep without a shepherd" (Matthew 9:36), stand up and remind yourself that Jesus is with you. Believe that he knows your troubles and is showering you with his compassion and his love.

You are not alone!

"Jesus, teach me how to cultivate your presence in myself and in the people around me."

October 6

That they may all be one. (John 17:21)

No person is the same as another. There's the tattoo-covered teenager down the street, the atheist coworker, the Christian relative from a different denomination.

How can Jesus possibly expect us to be one with all the "others" in our midst? By the power of the Holy Spirit, that's how!

One of the Spirit's greatest works is to create unity. The Spirit brought God and humanity together through the cross of Christ. He brought together Pharisees and tax collectors, Gentiles and Jews, centurions and fishermen, into one church in Jerusalem. The Spirit touched people's hearts and showed them how magnificent life could be as they came together in Christ.

Does unity mean everyone is identical? No! God created us as unique individuals, each with the ability to glorify him in our own way. He doesn't want us to be all the same.

Do you sense any judgment or envy in your thoughts toward people who are different than you? Ask the Spirit to replace those thoughts with love.

"Holy Spirit, teach me how to join in the prayer of Jesus. Lord, make us all one!"

October 7

Unless your faith is firm,
you shall not be firm! (Isaiah 7:9)

Faith matters! Faith sets the foundation of our lives, just as a house's foundation provides a solid footing for the building and a safe environment for the people who live there. Our faith in Jesus can do the same for us. It grounds us so that we can live with hope, even in the most challenging of environments.

Faith equips us to meet tough situations with peace and remain on the path of obedience. Best of all, it brings us joy and comfort because it tells us that God is with us and that our difficulties are never the end of the story.

God says to us, "Stand firm in your faith!" God has an answer for any challenge we face, and we can trust that it's the best answer possible.

"Jesus, I believe that you are with me. Help me stand firm in my faith today."

October 8

Joseph her husband, since he was a righteous man, . . .
decided to divorce her quietly. (Matthew 1:19)

Joseph could have told everyone in Nazareth that Mary was pregnant. Why didn't he? Let's focus on the word "quietly." Scripture tells us that he was a righteous man who listened to God and humbly followed him. So he sought to act in a way that upheld the dignity of Mary.

Today we have many opportunities to gripe about various injustices or troubling situations. It's very easy to lash out without thinking, but Joseph shows us that we don't have to succumb to such temptations. We can take the time to reflect on the situation and then act with discretion and tact.

What matters is that you seek to resolve troubling, difficult, or unexpected situations quietly and unobtrusively. When you act out of a rush of emotion instead of discretely, you risk making a mess of a situation that could have been settled much more lovingly and peacefully.

So before you react, take a breath and come before the Lord. Quietly reflect on what has happened. Ask God to give you strength. Then trust that God will show you how to act in a way that brings his love and peace.

"Lord, we look to you for the quiet strength to accomplish your will, even amid chaos."

October 9

Blessed are the peacemakers,
for they will be called children of God. (Matthew 5:9)

Have you ever met someone who has a knack for putting people at ease? When everyone else is arguing, they are calm. When everyone else is reacting, they are peacefully sizing up the situation. They seem to know how to defuse tension and get people talking to each other.

How can you be an agent of Jesus' peace?

First, and most important, pause to pray. You might say, "Lord, help me keep my emotions under control. Guard my thoughts and my speech. Fill me with your peace."

Second, listen. Consider what may be behind a person's words. Many disagreements can be resolved by hearing the other person's views.

Finally, speak positively. If someone is angry, let them know that you understand their feelings. If someone is troubled, offer to pray with them. If someone disagrees with you, seek common ground instead of highlighting your differences.

You can take small steps that will make a big difference in bringing the peace of Christ into the world.

"Lord, make me a peacemaker."

October 10

*I am creating new heavens
and a new earth. (Isaiah 65:17)*

God is never finished creating! He makes new things every day. Plants are pollinated and multiply; seeds mature into berries; volcanic lava creates new land formations. The world shifts and changes as God continues his active, creative work around us.

God is also creating in the spiritual world. Every day he creates new openings for you to receive his love and to experience healing and grace in your relationships. Every day he opens new doors by which you can share your faith. These are manifestations of the new creation that God is forming in and around you.

Where do you feel a bit new?

Where do you see new seeds about to blossom?

When it comes to matters of the heart, God is infinitely creative. He knows where you need renewal—in your prayer life, in your habits, in troubling relationships—and he is working to bring it about.

"Father, help me recognize your ongoing, creative work in me."

October 11

Remain in me, as I remain in you. (John 15:4)

Jesus tells us that he is the vine and we are the branches. Only as we are attached to him, receiving his vitality, are we fruitful.

Sometimes we get this confused. "God sent Jesus to redeem us," we think. "Now it's up to us." While this approach may sound noble, it can disconnect us from the Lord. And that will render us fruitless.

We all want to be useful to the Lord, to be filled with his vitality, his energy, and his wisdom. This is why it's important to be faithful to daily prayer, Scripture reading, connections with fellow Christians, and service. These things on their own won't bring spiritual growth, but they will keep us connected to the life-giving vine.

Try your best to stay close to Jesus. Give his Spirit the freedom to shape you and change you. You will become more fruitful!

Jesus, how would you want me to think and act today?

"Thank you, Jesus, for promising to make me fruitful. Help me, Lord, to stay connected to you."

October 12

The time of pruning the vines has come.
(Song of Songs 2:12)

When we think about being pruned, our reaction may be to hide. But Jesus reassures us: "Let me see your face, / let me hear your voice, / For your voice is sweet, / and your face is lovely" (Song of Songs 2:14).

A gardener prunes his plants to maximize their health as well as their yield. Jesus wants to prune away the parts of us that are not alive. Then, we can grow and change to be more like him.

Let's come into the light of our Lord's love. As we open our hearts to him, he can show us what needs to be pruned. Then we can live as beloved and cleansed children of God, ready to bear fruit for his kingdom!

Do you have the strength and courage to make some life changes? Will you go to Jesus for pruning?

"Jesus, lover of my soul, thank you for your unconditional love. Cleanse me, so that I can bear bountiful fruit for you."

October 13

Every tree is known by its own fruit. (Luke 6:44)

No matter how hard a tree may try, it cannot push its fruit to grow any faster than it was meant to grow. The tree's only job is to stay planted in the ground, draw water and nutrients from the soil, and receive the rays of the sun. The fruit then comes naturally.

As with a fruit seed, it is the nature of the spiritual seed planted in our hearts to bear fruit.

Have I allowed the seed of faith to take root in me?

What a joy to know that Jesus is fully committed to planting and bearing fruit in us! He has laid us in the perfect ground: his cross and resurrection. What's more, he has given us the Holy Spirit to guide us and teach us. As we listen to the Spirit and do as he asks, we become fruitful.

What does being fruitful mean to you?

Open your heart to Jesus. You'll be amazed at how he transforms you.

"Holy Spirit, you are the source of life. Help me remain in you and bear good fruit for you."

October 14

The fruit of the Spirit is love, joy, peace. (Galatians 5:22)

Imagine that your heart is an orchard. Picture yourself walking through that orchard with Jesus. As you walk, Jesus looks very happy. How can he not see the scraggly bushes sticking out—the moments of pride or moodiness, of hurting your neighbor's feelings?

But Jesus is enjoying the walk. He points out all the fruit he sees: you held your tongue with a coworker, helped a neighbor, and are serving your family. As you see this orchard through his eyes, you are amazed at how much fruit there is.

Yes, he sees the occasional weed. "Let me help you pull that out," he tells you. "I love you, and I see that you are welcoming the power of my cross and the grace of my indwelling Spirit. Keep it up, and you will bear much more fruit."

How does your heart feel now?

"Lord, I surrender to your Spirit. Help me follow you every day, so that I can produce more fruit through your work in my heart."

October 15

Of its own accord the land yields fruit. (Mark 4:28)

The farmer plants a seed, but it takes the right combination of soil, water, and God's grace to yield the "largest of plants" (Mark 4:32). And most of the work happens underground!

The same is true in the kingdom of God and in our own spiritual life. God works beneath the surface. He provides the nourishment of his grace so that we can blossom. Yes, we need to cooperate with that grace, but our growth will far outstrip our efforts.

God's work often happens unnoticed, so we should be careful to water the seed of faith even when we don't see impressive results. We can trust that God will bring the growth in his time and in his fashion.

Imagine yourself as that farmer.

Every time you pray, you're going to the well to get water. Every time you repent, you're improving the soil. As you come closer to Jesus, growth occurs.

God is making you holy!

"Lord, I trust you to bring about my growth. Help me cooperate with your work of grace."

October 16

The days will come when the bridegroom is taken away from them, and then they will fast. (Matthew 9:15)

Jesus is not asking us to mourn for him, as if he were gone forever. He wants us to be watchful and ready for the day when he returns!

Just as wedding guests are focused on the ceremony and the party afterward, we should keep our eyes fixed on Jesus' return.

Think about all that God has planned for you in heaven, on top of everything he has already given you in his Son. His heavenly banquet will be far more satisfying than the fanciest meal you could buy. This is a meal that he is anxious for you to taste, so don't pass on his offer!

Open your heart, and make room for Jesus. You have his invitation—signed with his sacrifice. What else can you say in response but "Here I am . . . I delight to do your will" (Psalm 40:7-8, NRSV)?

"Lord, help me keep my gaze on you. The more I look at you, the less everything else matters. May I desire nothing but to please you."

October 17

This is my prayer: that your love may increase ever more and more. (Philippians 1:9)

Judging from his Letter to the Philippians, it's likely that Paul saw the beginnings of division in the church there. He sought to put out the sparks as soon as he could. We can apply his wise words to our own lives.

How can we increase our love?

First, identify any sparks of disunity in your relationships. Then move on to putting out such sparks: getting up early to make the coffee at home; being kinder to the person sitting next to you at work; being patient with the driver ahead of you.

Even a smile can work wonders. Research shows that smiling can improve marriages and reduce stress. As Mother Teresa once said, "Every time you smile at someone, it is an action of love."

Pray, and trust that God will bring the "fruit of righteousness" to whatever good you do (Philippians 1:11).

"Lord, guide me in what I do each day, so that I can build up the people around me. Help me bear the fruit of righteousness."

October 18

*The field is the world, the good seed the
children of the kingdom. (Matthew 13:38)*

Sometimes gardeners deliberately plant different kinds of
vegetables very close together: peppers with carrots or
beans with tomatoes. Such "companion plants" help each
other grow. One might keep pests away, while the other offers
shade from the heat.

Think of how this analogy applies to you and your
relationships.

God's children are sown in close proximity as well—and
not always next to saints! God's plan is that in scattering
the seeds of his kingdom, he spreads his gospel throughout
the world.

Where has God planted you?

We've all been "bedded" in a family. Maybe you're also
sown into relationships within the corporate world or Little League baseball. Within these personal connections, God
wants you to be a means for the spread of his love.

Wherever you are, people can observe God's grace at work
within you. They notice your joy and kindness. God can speak
through you to help them grow closer to him. And remember, he will also use others to help you grow.

"Lord, use my life as a seed of your kingdom."

October 19

The sower sows the word. (Mark 4:14)

If there is one word that characterizes the sower in this parable, it is "generous." This fellow spreads his seeds everywhere. He doesn't seem all that concerned about where the seed will fall. He simply casts it to and fro.

How can we be generous, even indiscriminate, in sharing God's word and his promises? Whether the ground seems hard, weedy, thorny, or fertile, let us remember that it is the Lord who gives the growth (see 1 Corinthians 3:6-7). All we have to do is sow as generously as we can—in our words and in our actions, with both friends and strangers alike.

The world, the flesh, and the devil are sowing seeds all around us! How much more should we counter with the seeds of the gospel!

How will you sow today? What opportunities will you seize to spread the gospel?

Ask the Lord to help you see ways you can creatively witness to his love. He calls us to proclaim the word, in season and out!

"Lord Jesus, make me a generous evangelizer and sower of your word. Fill me with zeal and courage to spread your seeds all over the world!"

October 20

*Those who had been scattered went
about preaching the word. (Acts 8:4)*

Persecution of the Christians in Jerusalem heated up, and many of them scattered throughout the Mediterranean. You could say that the Lord used the evil intended to destroy the Church as a catalyst to make it spread farther. The result no doubt surprised the persecutors—and probably those who were being persecuted as well!

God wants to surprise us too. He wants to bring good out of whatever challenges we face. Those situations that get uncomfortably hot for us don't have to destroy us; instead they can help us grow. As St. Paul said, they can build our endurance, which builds our character, which in turn builds our hope (see Romans 5:3-4). And with stronger hope, we become stronger witnesses—as happened with the first disciples.

If you stay close to the Lord, no heat will consume you. And you may find opportunities to spread the warmth of God's love to the people around you.

"Father, I trust in you! When situations challenge me, help me remember that you will never abandon me."

October 21

Let perseverance be perfect. (James 1:4)

Being able to stay the course when things get difficult is often the deciding factor between success and failure. In fact, James equates perseverance with perfection. He writes that we should "consider it all joy" when trials allow us to grow in perseverance (James 1:2).

It can be hard to persevere. How do we stay the course?

How do we move forward in trust and confidence when our faith is tested?

We can take our cue from Jesus. He walked from village to village, with nowhere to lay his head. He was jostled by crowds and attacked by religious leaders. But he kept going—all the way to the end, to his death on the cross.

We have to keep going, as Jesus did. And we can trust that the grace that empowered him will keep us moving.

Pray for the grace to persevere through your own trial; pray too for Christians throughout the world who need that same grace. Then take comfort in knowing that many people are lifting you up right now, just as you are doing for them!

"Jesus, help me persevere through all the difficulties I encounter today."

October 22

The seed would sprout and grow,
he knows not how. (Mark 4:27)

A farmer can't predict his harvest from just planting seeds. Similarly, when we're working on one thing, God might be doing something else in our hearts, creating something new that we can't recognize until we look back and see it.

This means that we can relax a bit. While trying to stay vigilant at avoiding sin and growing in virtue, let it be a confident, happy vigilance, secure in the knowledge that God will bring growth where you need it the most. Plant your seeds and tend your garden as you think best, and know that your heavenly Father will bring his good work to completion in you (see Philippians 1:6).

God doesn't always show us what he is doing in our lives. Let us devote ourselves simply to loving him, loving our neighbors, and helping the needy. We can rest assured that our heavenly Father will take care of everything else!

"Lord, thank you for having an awesome plan for my life—
even if I can't see it all. Help me trust you day by day."

October 23

*Seeing . . . a fig tree in leaf, [Jesus] went over to
see if he could find anything on it. (Mark 11:13)*

What do fig trees and God's grace have in common?

They both bear fruit; it's in their natures. Jesus was
looking for figs even though "it was not the time for figs"
(Mark 11:13). His disciples might have been puzzled, but
over time they understood: if it's in your nature to be fruitful, you're going to bear fruit.

God wants all of us to produce fruit, in season and out of
season. The good news is that he's not sitting back waiting
for us to do so. He constantly pours his grace into us, giving
us what we need to do his work.

You are probably bearing spiritual fruit already: when
you're patient with your children, when you provide for your
family, when you comfort a friend, even when you let another
driver merge in front of you. You are doing good deeds.

You have received grace from God, empowering you to
bear fruit. What does your fruit look like?

*"Lord, thank you for giving me your grace. Help me recognize
this grace and bear fruit for your kingdom."*

October 24

Even if you do not believe me, believe the works.
(John 10:38)

Wherever he went, Jesus healed the sick, cast out demons, multiplied food, and raised the dead. Jesus' Spirit lives in us, so we too can live in holiness and do the things that he did.

God wants to use us to build his kingdom. People need to know his love and power. Many are suffering from wounds—spiritual, physical, and emotional—and God calls us to offer his healing touch.

We can do great things for God simply by loving the people close to us. Love is the foundation of everything Jesus did, and so it should be for us. We might pray for someone who is sick or hurting in some way—perhaps someone who feels discouraged or bitter.

Put aside any thoughts that you are unworthy or incapable. Press on in faith. All it takes to be an instrument of Jesus' healing, restoring touch is a little courage, a little prayer, and a healthy dose of God's grace.

"Lord, use me to build your kingdom."

October 25

Paul . . . found some disciples. (Acts 19:1)

The apostle Paul traveled from town to town so that he could be close to many new believers. The disciples in Ephesus hadn't yet heard about Jesus' resurrection or his gift of the Holy Spirit. They needed someone like Paul to come close to them, pray with them, and share what he knew.

In the world today, there are many different philosophies and religious ideas, distractions in the media, and demands on people's lives. Encounters with sincere, loving followers of Jesus can cut through that interference. You can be that connection of faith for people.

And you don't always have to say anything! Mowing a neighbor's lawn, smiling at a passerby, listening to a troubled friend—these are only a few ways to reach out.

Amid this busy, noisy, windy world, you have a powerful message. The witness of your life and the story of your journey can touch people's hearts and bring them closer to the Lord.

Don't be afraid to share it!

"Holy Spirit, help me draw closer to people and share my story with them."

October 26

My Lord and my God! (John 20:28)

St. Thomas, often known as "Doubting Thomas," may be one of the unsung heroes of the New Testament. One of the most profound acts of faith in the Gospels is his personal acclamation, "My Lord and my God!" These words were the fruit of all the time he had spent with Jesus and his determination to listen to Jesus and follow his lead.

Thomas was the first apostle to state his willingness to accompany Jesus even if it meant death (see John 11:16). He was also hungry to learn, asking at the Last Supper, "Master, we do not know where you are going; how can we know the way?" (14:5). Like the other disciples, after Pentecost Thomas traveled far and wide preaching the good news.

Jesus used Thomas to change the world. Maybe we should call him "Believing Thomas" or "Faithful Thomas" or "Adventurous Thomas."

Ask Jesus to give you the zeal and inquisitiveness and courage that this apostle had. You can be "blessed" even if you "have not seen and have believed" (John 20:29).

"Jesus, teach me to believe; then send me out as your witness."

October 27

Those who err in spirit shall acquire understanding.
(Isaiah 29:24)

Among the grand promises that will accompany our redemption is the gift of understanding. And what a gift this is!

To understand is to "stand under." It is to offer people support and to look at them with respect. Everyone is made in the image of God. This may be hard to detect in some, but the Lord can open our eyes to discern his handiwork. And that will lead us to understand people better.

Jesus demonstrates this kind of understanding in his encounters in the Gospels. He speaks personally to those who come for healing, acknowledging their faith. He connects with them and meets their needs.

Perhaps someone needs your understanding. Pray for an awareness of what you can respect in this person and how you might help them. Perhaps all Jesus wants from you is a listening ear and a sympathetic heart.

The gift of understanding can transform both that person and you!

"Jesus, thank you for understanding me, for supporting me, and for respecting me. Help me extend that understanding to others."

October 28

All creation is groaning in labor pains even until now.
(Romans 8:22)

Groaning is a natural response when something goes wrong. What does this tell you about a situation? And more importantly, what does your groaning move you to do?

Groaning is a sign that, deep down, we recognize that all is not as it should be. We have an inner sense of the glory that God wants us to experience, and we know that we fall short of that glory.

We don't yet experience the fullness of the life for which we were made.

Groaning is also a sign of hope! Like a woman in labor, we expect a wonderful glory that we do not yet see. There is more of the kingdom yet to be built, and we long to see it.

Use your groan as a springboard for action. And rejoice! God is at work in you. You are undergoing the birth of a new life in the glory of heaven. That's worth a few groans, isn't it?

"Lord Jesus, I want to see the glory you have for me!"

October 29

God is able to make every grace abundant for you, so that in all things, always having all you need, you may have an abundance for every good work. (2 Corinthians 9:8)

One mistake common to many beginning gardeners is to underestimate the zucchini they plant. Just one seed can produce up to nine pounds of food. So planting just a couple of seeds can result in a zucchini avalanche that leaves a gardener scrambling for clever recipes. Zucchini bread. Zucchini pizza. Chocolate zucchini cake.

This idea of a few seeds yielding an overwhelmingly large harvest is an appropriate analogy to kingdom life. God's abundant grace and mercy can lead us to reap much more than we sow. Every prayer asking God for his help, every act of kindness, every decision to forgive—they can produce baskets of blessings for the people around us.

So don't shy away from the opportunities that present themselves to you today. Remember the zucchini! Then go ahead and sow your seed.

"Lord, I believe that any seed of good I plant will be multiplied by your abundant grace. Give me the courage to continue to plant seeds and rejoice in your harvest."

October 30

Being examined . . . about a good deed done. (Acts 4:9)

Peter healed a beggar, and the people who witnessed the miracle were amazed. The Jewish rulers were offended, because Peter said that it was Jesus who healed the man—the Jesus whom they had crucified.

Unlike Peter, we will probably not be arrested for doing good deeds in the name of Jesus. But our good deeds will have an effect: often they will melt people's hearts and help them believe that God's love is real and powerful.

Ask Jesus to fill you with his love. His love is the catalyst that can move you to love and serve those around you. Then be as generous as you can. Be on the lookout for opportunities.

Jesus wants us to do good deeds. We may not have Peter's courage, but we all know how to do random acts of kindness. Make it a point to be cordial, helpful, generous, and compassionate.

Your acts of love are infectious. They may draw some people closer to God!

"Lord, fill me with your love. Inspire me to do good deeds for others."

October 31

Great are the works of the Lord. (Psalm 111:2)

That you are reading this meditation is a work of the Lord. That you know him at all is his work. That you acknowledge him, praise him, and worship him is his work. That you spend time in his presence is his work. That you repent and accept his forgiveness—this too is his work.

Great are these works: perfect and delightful, beautiful and intricate! Who can change his own heart or procure grace for himself? The best we can do is humbly receive all that God offers us and rejoice in the grace that is the hallmark of our lives.

You are always in God's thoughts. You occupy a special place in his heart. Even before you were born, he knew you and loved you. To this day, he cherishes and delights in you!

God is for you, and his word is always at work in you. So too is his great power, through which he does vastly more than you can ask or imagine. Give thanks then!

"Father, great are your works in and through me. Thank you for your goodness and kindness, today and always!"

Notes

November

LET US
GIVE THANKS!

November 1

I will maintain my covenant between me and you and your descendants after you. (Genesis 17:7)

O Lord, in every generation you have revealed yourself to your people. You have been faithful to your promises.

With the disobedience of our first parents, you promised to restore us to yourself. You chose Abraham to be our father in faith and made an everlasting covenant with him. You rescued us from slavery through your servant Moses.

Time and again your people forgot your covenant, and you remained faithful. Through the prophets you persistently called us back to you. You promised to give us a new heart and place a new spirit within us.

When the time was right, you made a new covenant in the blood of your Son. We were reconciled to you, and you gave us the promise of everlasting life. Your grace is constantly available to us—to enlighten us, strengthen us, and draw us to your side.

Father, you have never failed us!

"Faithful and awesome God, thank you! I want to respond by loving you, serving you, and trusting you all the days of my life."

November 2

Be very careful not to forget the things your own eyes have seen, nor let them slip from your heart as long as you live.
(Deuteronomy 4:9)

Isn't it amazing how easy it can be to forget, in the day-to-day grind, all that God has done for us?

It's helpful to step back and review both our personal history and the sweep of salvation history.

Make a list of times when you saw God working. Maybe he helped you address a wounded relationship. Maybe a time of prayer made you feel especially close to the Lord.

If you set these blessings firm in your memory, you will be able to draw on them in times of challenge. When you find yourself questioning God's love, they can help you dispel the doubt. When you are burdened by a trial, you can remember that God is with you, guiding you by his unseen hand.

Never let his blessings "slip from your memory"!

"Jesus, what a gift to be with you each day! Burn into my memory the great things you have done and are doing in my life."

November 3

Let the earth bless the Lord,
praise and exalt him above all forever. (Daniel 3:74)

Many people love to be outdoors, especially if we have spent a long time stuck at home or cooped up in an office. There's something in the natural world that revives our spirits. The beauty around us wakes up our senses in a way nothing else can. You could almost say that nature is speaking to us—but what is it saying?

All of nature is blessing God. The rain and snow, light and darkness, lightnings and clouds, the earth and the sky—all tell us of his beauty, his power, his closeness, and his humility.

When we glorify God, we see how wonderful he is. Jesus has redeemed us, our heavenly Father holds us in his hands, and the Holy Spirit lives in our hearts. The joy and confidence this gives us show that this is the way we were made to be: God-centered.

We can thank and praise God not just for the blessings he has given us but for the big blessings of forgiveness, redemption, and salvation. Praise him for his love. Adore him for his beautiful creation. Exalt him for his mercy.

"Lord, I contemplate your glory. Thank you for your grace and blessing in my life. Thank you for your redemption!"

November 4

Elisha the prophet had an open invitation to stay with a woman and her husband whenever he was in town. Grateful for their hospitality, Elisha prayed, and God gave the couple a child.

Scripture is clear that we are saved by Jesus alone, not by our actions. But it's also clear that God rejoices when we give our time, our treasure, and our talents in service to his people. Our acts of generosity move his heart, and he responds by pouring out his grace.

Our generosity is a response of thanks, a reflection of the good God has done for us. Our giving can show the world what God's generosity looks like. It can bring his love to them.

How can you thank God for all the good he has done for you?

Be a loving witness to the people around you. The Lord rejoices in whatever you do for him.

"Lord, show me how to be a witness of generous love."

November 5

Jonah made ready to flee to Tarshish. (Jonah 1:3)

God told Jonah to go preach to the sinful city of Nineveh. Jonah resisted God's call and boarded a ship going in the opposite direction. He ended up in the belly of a huge fish, floating precariously between life and death.

Have you ever felt a nudge from God that you didn't act on?

As far as Jonah was concerned, the Ninevites didn't deserve to hear the good news of God's mercy. He would have been happy to see them suffer God's wrath. God was being too soft, Jonah thought.

Those whom we might dismiss as unworthy can surprise us. They might convict us of our own need for deeper compassion and love. They also show us how merciful Jesus is toward us.

Jesus could have passed us by. He could have run the other way when confronted with our sin. But he rescued us. He became one of us and poured out his life for us. This is the best thing that could have ever happened to us.

Praise and thank the Lord for saving you. Then go and be an instrument of his mercy to everyone you meet!

"Jesus, thank you for loving and forgiving me!"

November 6

I will bless the Lord at all times. (Psalm 34:2)

Yes, Lord, I will bless you, because you are good, and everything you do is good.

Please fill me with your love. Please satisfy me with your peace and joy.

Lord, when I call to you for help, hear my every word, even the most hesitant whisper of my heart. When I am in trouble or pain, please comfort me. When sorrow darkens my heart, come to me and lift anxiety from me and hold me close.

Lord, you stay near to me, even though I don't always know it. Please listen to my prayer and act in your own wisdom and timing. Lift me up when sin makes me stumble. Redeem me from death and made me yours forever.

How gracious you are, Lord! You take delight in saving the people you love, even when they have wandered from you.

Thank you, Jesus! What a blessing to be able to turn to you! What joy it is to know you!

"Lord, I praise you and thank you for your goodness! I will bless you, Lord, at all times."

November 7

We too give thanks to God unceasingly.
(1 Thessalonians 2:13)

We all have good days and bad days. Sometimes we are filled with thanksgiving and joy, and other times we find life a struggle. In the challenging times, it can be helpful to remember that other people are thankful for us.

If St. Paul were talking to you today, he would probably be giving thanks for you. He would tell you how proud he is of the way you are pursuing the Lord. He would see your meditating on God's word as a sign that you are holding fast to your faith. He might even rejoice in God's ability to keep you on the right path.

Your spouse, your family, and your fellow believers are all grateful for your perseverance and your support to them. The Lord especially is delighted that you are following him! You are precious to him and vital to his kingdom.

So keep on keeping on!

"Lord, thank you for all the people who have gone before me and all those around me. Thank you for their support and their prayers."

November 8

Blessed [are] those who keep his testimonies,
who seek him with all their heart. (Psalm 119:2)

What does it mean to be blessed? According to the dictionary, it means to be "divinely or supremely favored." According to popular culture, you are blessed if you have lots of possessions or are in good health. But God sees blessing differently.

God cares about our physical lives, but his greatest blessings are more spiritual than material. The Israelites were blessed to be God's people. Jesus taught that everyone who heard the word of God and obeyed it was blessed (see Luke 11:28). St. Paul declared blessed those whose sins are forgiven (see Romans 4:7). And the apostle John said that those who "wash their robes" and eat from the "tree of life" are blessed (Revelation 22:14).

Think about all the ways that God blesses you. He shows his peace and presence when you turn to him in the midst of difficulties. He gives you strength to forgive others. He gives you grace to turn away from temptations. All these, and many more, are clear blessings from the Lord!

"Lord, how generous you are! Help me see the blessings you have lavished on me. Teach me how to remain open to all the blessings you want to pour on me today."

November 9

Sin lies in wait at the door. (Genesis 4:7)

Cain felt slighted because Abel enjoyed God's favor while he did not. Yet God was very good to Cain. Not only did he warn him about the dangers of jealousy; he also treated him with mercy after Abel's death (see Genesis 4:15).

In our competitive world, there are plenty of opportunities to get beat out at something. It could be as major as not getting hired or as minor as getting cut off in traffic. We can choose to feel resentful or to relax, knowing that God will give us everything we need.

The best way to counter jealousy, or any kind of discontent, is to give thanks for what we already have . . . the very best thing being the love of Jesus. Nothing can take that away from us!

As you take ten minutes each day praising and thanking God for his love and blessings, you'll find your outlook changing.

You are a child of God, and in him, you have everything. Make thanksgiving your way of life, and you'll be in great shape!

"Jesus, thank you for your love! Thank you for never failing me, even when I've failed you. Your grace is all that I will ever need."

November 10

Blessed are the clean of heart,
for they will see God. (Matthew 5:8)

The cleanliness of which Jesus speaks is not something we can attain on our own. It's a gracious gift from him. He cleansed us of original sin and continues to wash us clean of the sins we commit. He cleanses our consciences every time we turn to him in prayer and ask his pardon. Over and over, his grace reaches down to our souls and offers us a new start.

Do you need a new start?

Jesus tells us that we who are cleansed will see God! Think of the many people who have gone before you, all those who have been purified in the blood of the Lamb. Imagine them in heaven, caught up in worship, filled with the love of the Lord. Then picture yourself there with them.

This is Jesus' promise to everyone who seeks purity of heart. Let the Lamb of God cleanse you. Stay close to him, and you will end up worshipping him with the great multitude!

"Blessing and glory, wisdom and thanksgiving,
honor, power, and might
be to our God forever and ever." (Revelation 7:12)

November 11

Who was I to be able to hinder God? (Acts 11:17)

Throughout salvation history, God's standard operating procedure is the unusual. Consider Noah, whom God told to build a boat in the middle of the desert. Or the elderly Abraham, being promised descendants as numerous as the stars. God brought down the mighty city of Jericho by having the Israelites march around the city seven times. Truly, God's ways are not our ways!

Peter testified to how unusual God's ways can appear. The other believers chastised him for eating with Gentiles, an action unthinkable for a devout Jew. God showed Peter that salvation was meant for all peoples. What could Peter do but follow this directive?

How easy it can be to put God in a box. He can do "far more than all we ask or imagine" (Ephesians 3:20). In fact, God delights in doing the unexpected. He takes joy in exceeding our wildest dreams.

Think of all the unexpected ways God has acted in your life. Then thank him for his blessings.

"Thank you, Lord, for all the pleasant surprises and wonderful lessons you have given me. Jesus, I trust in you."

November 12

If the Lord wills it, we shall live to do this or that.
(James 4:15)

We might assume that James is addressing an attitude of presumptuousness: some of his readers seem to be "doing this or that" without paying attention to the spiritual ramifications of their actions. We know that God doesn't want us to be super spiritual or fearful or apathetic. So how should we read this passage?

Perhaps we can look at the sentence in reverse: we live to do "this or that" because the Lord wills it. This reminds us that every moment of our life is a gift, held in place by God, and the right response is to be thankful. The remedy for presumptuousness is humility and gratitude.

Let gratitude take root in your heart today. Give thanks for the challenges that God has allowed in your life. They have helped make you who you are.

Give thanks too for the present moment, which is also filled with God's presence. And give thanks for a future you can be hopeful about, because your heavenly Father holds your whole life in his hands!

"Lord, thank you for the generosity of your will."

November 13

Lead me in the path of your commandments,
for that is my delight. (Psalm 119:35)

Rarely do people say that they delight in commands, particularly at the moment they are given. One possible exception is guidance by a revered mentor.

The psalmist recognizes that God is the perfect mentor. This divine teacher knows our strengths and weaknesses and how to help us along. God's plans are only for our good; they are lovingly designed to put us on the path to happiness.

We don't have an absentee father! Almighty God walks beside us every day, always ready to help us. He is committed to keeping us on the right path and showing us how to delight in his ways.

What "command" might God want you to delight in today?

To serve your family?

To spend time with him in prayer?

To forgive someone who has hurt you?

Embrace this command, confident in your Father's power to transform you.

"Father, thank you for leading me on the path of your commands. Teach me, mold me, and empower me, so that I can find delight in your will."

November 14

The grace of our Lord has been abundant.
(1 Timothy 1:14)

How often do you stop and review the sins of your past, especially the sins you have already confessed and put behind you? Have you ever considered looking back instead at how God has changed your life?

"I was once a blasphemer . . . and an arrogant man," Paul tells his friend Timothy, "but I have been mercifully treated. . . . The grace of our Lord has been abundant" (1 Timothy 1:13, 14).

Consider the abundance of God's grace in your life. Maybe you have grown closer to Jesus in your prayer. Maybe he has helped you overcome anger, laziness, or pride. Maybe you received grace to forgive someone. Chances are that God's grace has been powerful, persistent, and unconditional.

Like Paul, you have been "mercifully treated" to God's never-ending, overflowing grace (1 Timothy 1:13). This is an invitation to praise and thanksgiving.

Thank God for his grace, for his work in you. Rejoice in how far you've come in grace, and let God move you to even more.

"Jesus, thank you for your abundant grace in my life. Help me become more like you!"

November 15

He makes his sun rise on the bad and the good, and causes rain to fall on the just and the unjust.
(Matthew 5:45)

Hang on a minute! Isn't that unfair? Why don't the good and the just get special treatment? At the very least, the bad and the unjust should get the shorter end of the stick. If God is perfectly just, then shouldn't that be the way things go?

Well, not really. God's justice encompasses something much more profound than a heavenly balance sheet. And that's a good thing for us. For in the end, we are all sinners, aren't we?

Thank God that his justice, his wisdom, and all his attributes find their perfection in his love. It is love that makes him merciful to those who don't deserve it, including you!

He loves you and calls you his child despite your sin. This is the triumph of divine love, the perfection of God's justice!

Look to the sky. If it's sunny, praise the Lord for shining on everyone—good and bad. If it's rainy, thank him for bringing refreshing nourishment to everyone—saint and sinner. He is a merciful, loving, gracious God, and he wants to bless all of us!

"Father, I thank you for your mercy! May your love fill me to overflowing, that I can share it with everyone around me."

November 16

We hold this treasure in earthen vessels.
(2 Corinthians 4:7)

Today, an inspiring prayer of thanks:

Praise to our Lord Jesus for pouring the treasure of divine life into the "earthen vessels" of our all-too-mortal lives! Sin might lurk in our hearts and even leap out at times; we turn to Jesus and are made new.

Thank you, Jesus, for shining your light into our lives! Thank you for nailing our sin to the cross. Thank you for cleansing us by your blood and offering us your own risen life. Thank you for letting us experience God's love so intimately.

Jesus has freed us from a life of self-reliance. We praise him even for the times when we feel "perplexed, but not driven to despair; . . . struck down, but not destroyed" (2 Corinthians 4:8, 9), for those are the times when he pours out gifts of forgiveness and life eternal!

Let us continue to surrender to Jesus. When we were without hope and without God, he saved us. Even now, in whatever situation we find ourselves, we know that he is with us and will show us the way.

"Lord, we join the hosts of heaven in grateful thanksgiving to you, our Savior!"

November 17

Oh, that today you would hear his voice:
Do not harden not your hearts. (Psalm 95:7-8)

"**I**s my heart hard or soft? Am I open to the Lord or just going through the motions?"

The psalmist offers us a strategy designed to keep our hearts soft.

Let us sing joyfully to the LORD (Psalm 95:1). Using our voices to honor the Lord helps us stay focused on him. Don't worry about sounding great. Another psalm even encourages us to "shout joyfully to the LORD" (Psalm 100:1).

Let us come before him with a song of praise (Psalm 95:2). Giving thanks to God helps us recognize that the Lord has provided for us. The food we eat, the clothes we wear, and even our friends and family are all gifts from the Lord. The more we remember this, the more inclined we will be to put God in a place of honor, to turn to him for help, and to listen to his word.

Let us bow down in worship (Psalm 95:6). We can kneel, lift our hands, or even dance as we pray. As we use our bodies to worship God, our hearts will follow suit.

"Lord, I worship you. Keep my heart soft, so that I can always hear you."

November 18

Do not be distressed. . . . It was really for the sake of saving lives that God sent me here ahead of you.
(Genesis 45:5)

Joseph's brothers sold him into slavery. Then his master's wife falsely accused him of molesting her. Even in prison, Joseph held firm to God. And God brought good out of evil—not only for Joseph but for all the people around him.

This is a classic story of good and evil: the goodness of Joseph contrasted with the evil done by others. Goodness eventually triumphs. As Paul wrote in Romans 8:28, "All things work for good for those who love God."

If we seek to do good and forgive those who harm us, miracles can happen—not only in our lives but in the lives of those around us. Let's face hard times with faith and trust in God's promises.

Who knows what blessings God has waiting for us?

"Father, I surrender my life into your hands. When I get weary of fighting the good fight, lift me up and hide me in your presence. Keep me safe until I am able to praise and thank you once again."

November 19

Give and gifts will be given to you; a good measure, packed together, shaken down, and overflowing, will be poured into your lap. (Luke 6:38)

Most toddlers have no trouble learning the meaning of "mine." They do, however, need to be taught how to share! As children mature, they begin to get the point that if they want to have any friends at all, they need to be flexible.

Unfortunately, the childish concept of "mine" often lingers into adult life. That's why Jesus spent so much time teaching and modeling for us another way—a way of selfless giving. In sermon after sermon, Jesus told us that the more we empty ourselves and give to other people, the more room we have to receive the good things that God has in store for us.

God's gifts include wisdom, discernment, patience, and evangelization. They can help us handle a family crisis and hold on to our faith when inconvenient things happen. As we give God room in our hearts, he pours grace into us.

Look up to heaven today, and fix your eyes on the Lord. Watch to see what gifts he pours into your life. Know too that the more you share those gifts, the more he will give to you.

"Merciful Father, I open my heart and receive all that you generously offer me. Help me be both a giver and a receiver of your goodness."

November 20

To Timothy, my dear child: grace, mercy, and peace from God the Father and Christ Jesus our Lord. (2 Timothy 1:2)

Paul's greeting expresses his love for his spiritual son and points Timothy's eyes to heaven. Paul reminds Timothy that God stands ready to fill him with spiritual blessings, to give him peace and an assurance of his love.

Grace is God's unmerited favor. Mercy is his gift of unlimited forgiveness. And peace is the gift that flows when we are open to receiving God's grace and mercy (see Ephesians 2:8-9; Hebrews 4:16; Ephesians 2:4-5; John 14:27). God isn't stingy with these gifts, and Paul wants Timothy to embrace them more deeply.

Grace, mercy, and peace flow constantly into us, day in and day out. They form a waterfall from heaven, a torrent always ready to flood our souls.

Imagine yourself standing under the waterfall of God's blessings. Splash about in them. Receive all the grace God has for you today. Rejoice in your good, generous, and loving God.

May grace, mercy, and peace be with you today.

"Thank you, Lord, for your superabundant blessings!"

November 21

*Beware that your hearts do not become drowsy from . . .
the anxieties of daily life. (Luke 21:34)*

You might not associate being anxious with being drowsy.
When you're anxious, you might feel jittery, even panicky, but not sleepy.

The drowsiness Jesus is talking about doesn't really have
to do with sleep. He's warning his disciples not to be careless, not to let anything turn their attention away from his
love and provision for them.

One of the best ways to shake off this type of drowsiness
is by being mindful of all the ways God is providing for you.

Gratitude is a habit you can develop with practice. For
example, you can write down things you are thankful for,
the wonders you have seen God do. "Thank you, Lord, for
the encouraging email from my friend." "Thank you, Lord,
for healing my cold."

Reading that list out loud in your prayer time will help
you form an attitude of thankfulness.

Gratitude is a great antidote to day-to-day anxieties. It
will make you alert to God's goodness and "wake you up"
to God's presence in your life!

"Lord, thank you for the many blessings of this week."

November 22

God shall give them light, and they shall reign forever and ever. (Revelation 22:5)

Are you one of those people who can't help but peek at the end of a book long before you actually get there? You know, the type who wants to know whether or not the good guys are going to win?

You might call John's vision in Revelation the happy ending to our story. The good guys—Jesus and his followers—do win in the end. This shows us where our lives are headed. It gives us hope and anticipation as we work through the ups and downs of life.

Imagine what that glorious day will be like! Let's praise God for all that he has planned for us: refreshment in "the river of life-giving water, sparkling like crystal" (Revelation 22:1); healing and strength from the "tree of life" (22:2); every tear wiped from our eyes; and no more "death or mourning, wailing or pain" (21:4)

Even "night will be no more" (22:5). No more confusion! No more temptation! No more darkness of guilt and sin! We will stand before the heavenly throne and see God face-to-face!

Let us thank the Lord for this vision and for walking with us here on earth toward our happy ending!

"Jesus, thank you for the promise of heaven! I trust in you."

November 23

The peace of God . . . will guard your hearts.
(Philippians 4:7)

There was once a little town that was being harassed and pillaged by marauders. Good families were not able to defend themselves. The town was filled with fear. The king was shocked to learn what was happening to his own citizens. He immediately dispatched soldiers to set up command posts at every town entry point. In short order, the raids came to an end, and peace came.

Likewise, God comes to our rescue. Paul says that if "with thanksgiving" we "make [our] requests known to God," we will know peace (Philippians 4:6).

How often do you bring your needs to the Lord in prayer? Probably quite a bit—especially the big concerns in your life. But Paul asks us to do that in a spirit of thanksgiving. He reminds us that our heavenly Father, who has counted every hair on our heads, knows us deeply and has nothing but good in mind for us.

God is inviting us to bring all our pain and anxiety to him, so that he can give us his guidance and his comfort. He wants us to be grateful that he is with us.

"Father, I trust in your love. Teach me the way of surrender, the way of peace."

November 24

They . . . returned to Jerusalem with great joy.
(Luke 24:52)

Surprisingly, Jesus' apostles do not weep when Jesus rose to heaven. Their display of exuberance can make them appear almost superhuman. Didn't they feel sad that Jesus decided to leave them?

Of course they were sad. But more than that, they were confident that they would one day follow where Jesus had gone. Their hope of seeing him again made their sorrow sweet.

This is the key to our joy as well. We know that Jesus has gone to prepare a place for us in heaven.

Think about how he has opened heaven to you, a place you could never reach on your own. Imagine him standing with his Father, your Father. See the smile on his face as he thinks about opening the doors to your new home and welcomes you in.

Jesus longs for all God's children to join him. He never stops interceding for us and pouring out grace—all so that we can one day taste the sweetness of heaven.

"Thank you, Jesus, for opening heaven for me!"

November 25

Enter his gates with thanksgiving. (Psalm 100:4)

At the center of Psalm 100 stands the unshakable foundation for our praise: the Lord is God, and we are his people. Our God is good; his love for us never wavers. He is always on our side, always rooting for us.

But what about us, the sheep of his flock? How do we respond? Sometimes faithful, sometimes wandering. Sometimes gorging ourselves, occasionally requiring restraint. Egging each other on until fear or fighting breaks out, yet vitally in need of each other.

Through it all, God is unfailingly good. Thus the psalmist urges us to approach the Lord with gladness, singing our thanks and praise.

Your God loves you. He loves to give you good things. He loves you so much that sometimes he restrains you. He calms you when panic strikes, and he will always defend you against whatever might prey on your soul.

God is the Good Shepherd who calls you by name. So sing joyfully to him! Praise and thank him for his kindness and faithfulness to you!

"God, you are good! When I wander, you remain faithful. When I follow, you lavish kindness on me. I praise you for your constant goodness!"

November 26

We always give thanks to God, the Father of our Lord Jesus Christ, when we pray for you. (Colossians 1:3)

Paul had a lot to pray for when it came to the believers in Colossae. False teachers were leading some astray. Paul needed to set the people straight.

But Paul doesn't begin his letter by drawing attention to the problems; instead he gives thanks. He thanks God for the Colossians' authentic faith, for their genuine love, and for the depth of their hope in the Lord.

Thanksgiving can help us focus our intercessory prayer. When we give thanks for all the good that God is already doing in a situation, our hope is built. Our confidence that he will intervene according to his own wisdom and timing gets a powerful boost.

As you pray, ask God to bring to light the good things he is already doing. Trust he will continue to help you. Let him show you that he is indeed trustworthy.

"Lord, you know the situations that weigh heavily on me. Open my eyes to the ways you are already at work, and help me be thankful."

November 27

The cloud filled the house of the LORD so that the priests could no longer minister . . . , since the glory of the LORD had filled the house of the LORD. (1 Kings 8:10-11)

Like the Israelites before the ark of the covenant, we can experience the glory of the Lord as we worship him with sincere hearts.

One way to worship is to take one of the many psalms of praise (such as Psalm 47, 66, 95, 100, or 150) and read it out loud, turning it into our own prayer of praise. We can speak out loud to the Lord in our own words, thanking him for sending his Son and the Holy Spirit and for Jesus' promise to come again in glory.

We can fill our homes with worship music, either by tuning in to a Christian radio station or streaming worship music, and let God speak to our hearts.

Just as the cloud of the Lord's glory filled the Temple, the joy and love of God will fill your home and your heart when God is worshipped there.

"Jesus, thank you for all the blessings you have given me and for all you have promised to do. May your glory fall on me and remain with me throughout the day."

November 28

Glory that surpasses . . . (2 Corinthians 3:10)

We have it all! We know the forgiveness of sins through Jesus Christ. We have received the Holy Spirit to strengthen us on the road to holiness; he helps us pray, turn back to God when we feel weak, and be thankful. The Scriptures teach us how to overcome temptation and be one body in Christ.

God's plan for us gets better and better as we grow closer to him and to our eternal destiny. And we know that God has still more for us.

When Jesus comes again in glory, all pain and suffering will be banished. Sickness will no longer affect us, and our bodies will be whole and radiant. We won't struggle with temptation. We will desire whatever God desires. In our heavenly home, we will experience total contentment.

We can be very grateful for the blessings we enjoy now. Still, it's exciting to think that God's plan for us will only get better. Come, Lord Jesus!

"Thank you, Lord, for your blessings today and for your promise of all that is to come!"

November 29

Your faith has saved you. (Luke 17:19)

The leper was an outcast: his body deformed, its stench repelling, no hope for a cure. His life was one of misery and decay.

Then he met Jesus, who sent him to the priests. As the leper obeyed, he realized that he was healed! Amazed and grateful, he ran back to Jesus, threw himself at his feet, and worshipped.

This story tells us what Jesus is looking for from all of us. When our prayers are answered, he wants us to thank and worship him—not because he loves being praised but because he knows that worship will build our faith. Every time we praise and thank him for his marvelous deeds, our hearts are softened, and we become more open to his word, his work, and his love.

Take time to thank God for grace-filled moments you have experienced.

Let this move you to deeper surrender to God. He will take you even further in faith.

"Lord, with all my heart I sing your praises. Thank you for turning my mourning into dancing and my tears into laughter."

November 30

Praise God. (Psalm 150:1)

The psalms tell of God's might, his faithfulness, and his mercy. Many of them urge us to praise the Lord in response. This final psalm tells us where, why, and how to praise the Lord, as well as who should be doing the praising.

Where are we to praise God? He is present in our churches, of course, but he is also in our homes and in the innermost part of our souls.

Why praise God? Because of his majesty and his mighty deeds. He has revealed himself as our Savior, healer, and restorer.

How should we praise? With music, singing, and even dancing. Our praise should fill the atmosphere!

Finally, who should praise God? "Everything that has breath" (Psalm 150:6)! This includes you.

Turn to the Lord in the innermost places of your heart. Call to mind how he has blessed you, loved you, guarded you, redeemed you, healed you, and transformed you. Find a way to praise him for all this. Sing a familiar hymn, offer a quiet prayer, or tell a friend about how good God has been to you.

"Lord, I praise you."

EMMANUEL,
GOD WITH US

December 1

The LORD comforts his people. (Isaiah 49:13)

When you think about being comforted, you might imagine someone putting their arms around you or speaking encouraging words when you were hurt or sick or upset. Even if you never knew this kind of comfort from people, you can experience it from God.

Your God knows you intimately; he created you. There isn't anything he doesn't know. He knows your needs, your worries, and your sorrows. He won't forget you, not even for an instant. Even if a mother forgets her child, God will never forget you (see Isaiah 49:15).

Now, you can't have someone's arm around you all the time. But then again, maybe you can. God's comfort is not limited to physical closeness. He is always with you, even when you make a mess of things. The Scriptures proclaim that he will be with us always—and he never breaks his promises (see Matthew 28:20).

God walks beside you: suffering with you, persevering with you, and comforting you. Talk to Jesus about your joys and struggles, your questions and doubts. It's in those moments that you may begin to sense his presence and his comfort.

"Jesus, be my comfort today."

December 2

You have approached Mount Zion. (Hebrews 12:22)

Blazing fire. Gloomy darkness. A trumpet blast. A voice that caused its hearers to beg for silence. The author of Hebrews goes so far as to warn us: "It is a fearful thing to fall into the hands of the living God" (Hebrews 10:31).

But this all-consuming fire is also our heavenly Father who waits patiently for us to come to him. The all-powerful creator is like the mother hen eager to gather us (see Matthew 23:37). The lawgiver is a lover pursuing his beloved across space and time (see Song of Songs 2:8-9).

Because of Christ, we are invited into a personal relationship with the God of the universe!

We can enjoy real, warm, personal companionship with the One who holds the keys to heaven and hell. Jesus' blood speaks a word of mercy and not vengeance (see Hebrews 12:24).

The Father wants a relationship of loving surrender and trust with you. Jesus stands at the door of your heart (see Revelation 3:20), calling you to deeper holiness and asking you to let him in.

Yes, you have come to Mount Zion—as an honored guest of the King of kings!

"Father, let me hear your voice today!"

December 3

The Lord is with you. (Luke 1:28)

In the Old Testament, God communicated mainly with Israel's leaders and prophets. Gabriel marked the beginning of a new relationship between God and his people. The uncreated, omnipotent God became Emmanuel, God with us.

For Mary, this meant the nearness of the Lord conceived in her womb. For Jesus' disciples, it meant an encounter with God made flesh. And for us, it means the presence of God dwelling in our hearts through the Spirit.

The Lord is with you. The angel's announcement rings down through the centuries to each of us. God is with us through every experience—the joyful moments, the sad ones, the difficult ones, and every moment in between. He is with us in our deepest spiritual experiences, and he is with us when we can't feel his presence at all.

Let this phrase remind you of God's presence. Let it be a comfort when you feel alone, an encouragement when you feel discouraged, and a blessing in times of joy. Jesus is always with you.

"Lord, thank you for being with me all the time."

December 4

The young woman, pregnant and about to bear a son, shall name him Emmanuel. (Isaiah 7:14)

God wanted to reassure King Ahaz that he was with him in Israel's struggles. The sign he gave was that a virgin was to bear a child—one who would be so filled with God's Spirit that people would call him Emmanuel, which is Hebrew for "God is with us."

In Nazareth, hundreds of years later, we see Mary saying yes to God's promise. The angel told her that she would become a mother by the power of God. She accepted God's word and went forward in faith and trust. She knew the Lord was trustworthy. "May it be done to me according to your word" (Luke 1:38).

Each day, we are challenged to embrace opportunities to grow in our faith.

That faith will give us the strength and the generosity to say a more complete yes to the God who is with us.

"Lord, thank you for all you have done to show me your presence and your love! Help me be confident in your commitment to me."

December 5

His dwelling shall be glorious. (Isaiah 11:10)

Who would have thought that Jesus would choose to make his glorious dwelling in a humble stable? No pomp. No fanfare. No royal attendants. His presence alone made that stable glorious.

Jesus continues to come to us in humility. He chooses to enter our ordinary circumstances and make them glorious. He embraces our highs and lows, triumphs and failures.

Jesus is happy to come to us: to our messy homes, to crying children, to difficult relationships, to prison cells and hospital rooms. He comes when we feel isolated or afraid, just as readily as he comes to families gathered around the table and worshippers gathered in a church. He comes in times of joy and times of sorrow and fills them with his glory. Jesus is always Emmanuel, God with us.

So don't be afraid to welcome Jesus. Don't think you're unworthy. Don't let shame or fear keep you from opening the door to him. He knows what it's like to live in an all-too-human, less-than-perfect world. Not only will he come into your home and your life, but he will change it—simply by his loving presence.

"Jesus, come and dwell in every part of my life. Make me into your glorious dwelling place."

December 6

Here is your God, . . .
he comes to save you. (Isaiah 35:4)

This joyful message of God's saving love came at a bleak moment in the history of his people. Judah had rebelled against the Lord and been taken into captivity by the Babylonians. At this low point in their history, God did not abandon them but promised to save them. He spoke tenderly to them: "The ransomed of the LORD shall return, / and enter Zion singing, / crowned with everlasting joy" (Isaiah 35:10).

God continues to pursue us. Even in the shadows of our messy lives, still God seeks us out to save us. Oftentimes he will join us in any mess we've made and help us clean it up!

The message of Christmas is that God never walks away from us. He is unconditionally devoted to us. Even when we sin, even when we get ourselves in trouble, we hear this joyful proclamation: "Here is your God." He comes to save us by becoming one of us. He is Emmanuel, God with us.

"Jesus, thank you for coming to redeem me. Lord, I rejoice in you!"

December 7

Is God indeed to dwell on earth? (1 Kings 8:27)

"If the heavens and the highest heavens cannot contain you," King Solomon asked, "how much less this house which I have built!" (1 Kings 8:27). The one who made the stars came to live in a building made of wood and stone. Why? What could be so compelling about this one spot in the universe?

There is one possible answer: love. It's the reason God created this world. He wanted a people with whom he could share his creative, overflowing love. He spoke his laws to his people, rescued them from slavery, and formed them through the prophets.

Then came the biggest blessing: God came to dwell, not just through his word, not just through historical events, not just through the beauty of creation, but as a human being, fully man and fully God. And now Jesus continues to dwell on earth by dwelling in us! He has made each of us into a temple of the Holy Spirit, more sacred than Solomon's Temple.

Let us stand amazed at God's goodness and generosity.

"Father, I marvel that you love me so deeply as to come to me. Give me a greater reverence for your presence in me—and in every single person you call your own."

December 8

In [God] our hearts rejoice. (Psalm 33:21)

Throughout Scripture it is evident that being in God's presence changes lives.

The Song of Songs tells us that God's love reaches deep into our hearts and fills us in a way that no other love can. The proclamations of praise and heartfelt cries found throughout the Book of Psalms flowed out of people's experiences of the Lord.

Even today, Jesus offers you the gift of his presence. He is waiting for you, eager to welcome you. It doesn't even matter what method you choose to come to him. You can find him in a multitude of ways: as you are dancing with praise music, chanting hymns, sitting in a chapel, or lying on your living room floor. You may experience him in a way different from your friend or even your spouse. But that doesn't matter. All that matters is that Jesus is right next to you, waiting to be found by you!

There is no better place to be than in the presence of Jesus, your Redeemer and friend!

"Lord Jesus, thank you for calling me to be with you. Thank you for the privilege of walking with you every day!"

December 9

Like a shepherd he feeds his flock. (Isaiah 40:11)

Isaiah depicts the ideal shepherd as tender and solicitous yet powerful. "In his arms he gathers the lambs, / Carrying them in his bosom" (Isaiah 40:11). This ideal shepherd "comes with power" and "rules by his strong arm" (40:10). He braves danger to defend the flock against predators.

In the following story, imagine yourself as one of the sheep.

Jesus is our Good Shepherd (see John 10:11). He doesn't wait anxiously for straying sheep to return but rather sets out in search of them. He rescues us from spiritual threats posed by the devil, our fallen nature, and darkened philosophies of the world.

Jesus' kindness might feel like discipline. He might cut a lamb loose from brambles, dress its wounds, and restrain it from wandering. He loves his sheep and knows what is best for them.

Ask the Holy Spirit to open your eyes to the depth and breadth of love that Jesus has for you. He is your Good Shepherd, and he has you in his arms.

"Jesus, thank you for seeking me when I stray from the path. Be my shepherd; keep me in your care."

December 10

I will turn ... the dry ground into springs of water.
(Isaiah 41:18)

Christmas is coming, and all those items on the to-do list might tempt us to skip our times with the Lord. Yet there is a thirst deep within us that only God can quench. The prophet Isaiah urges us to look to the Lord.

This busy season is a blessed time as well, for it's an opportunity to contemplate the faithfulness of God. He fulfilled his promise of a Messiah in the greatest possible way: by sending Jesus.

Start your day with the only task that will truly satisfy your heart: time with the Lord! Meditate on the wonder of the Incarnation, of God loving us so much that he became a man to save us.

Turn your gaze to the Lord throughout the day. Remember why you are buying gifts, making special foods, and decorating your home: so that you can welcome Jesus and rejoice in his coming!

"Jesus, I want to prepare for your coming this Christmas. Help me recognize my thirst for you, so that I can drink deeply of your love."

December 11

If only you would attend to my commandments . . .
(Isaiah 48:18)

Throughout Israel's history, God pleaded with his people to obey him. Now exiled in Babylon, would they finally do what God asked?

Perhaps the answer is in the previous verse: "I am the LORD, your God, / teaching you how to prevail" (Isaiah 48:17). If Israel would believe that God himself was speaking to them, they would see his commandments as words of wisdom and guidance—as laws that could give them peace.

What about us?

Let's ponder today how we can let God lead us. Jesus is with us every step of the way, and he has sent his Holy Spirit to live in our hearts. He wants to encourage us, give us his strength, and show us how deeply our Father loves us. He wants to teach us God's ways and pick us up whenever we fall.

God promises "prosperity . . . like a river" (Isaiah 48:18, NRSV) to those who obey him. Give the Lord room in your life. Sit at his feet, and let him take charge!

"Lord, let me hear your word in my heart, and let it transform me."

December 12

Are you the one who is to come? (Luke 7:19)

Miracles, signs, and wonders! What excitement John's two disciples must have experienced as they came to see for themselves what Jesus was doing!

We share this excitement as we anticipate Jesus' coming again in glory. We can also be excited at his coming into our hearts whenever we approach him in prayer.

Every time we pray, we can ask Jesus:

What do you want to do in my life today?

How will you answer my prayers?

What new insights do you have for me?

How will I experience your love, glory, or mercy today?

The Gospels show us how pleased Jesus was when people approached him with a lively and expectant faith. Seek him eagerly. Trust him. Let him know how much you enjoy his company and the wonders he is working in you and around you. Thank him for the infinite store of grace and blessings he has for you!

"Lord, I come to you with joy and excitement today. Reveal your wonders in my life as I surrender to you. Come and do whatever you want to deepen my faith in you!"

December 13

Be watchful! Be alert! (Mark 13:33)

God requests the honor of your presence at the entry of his Son into the world. This event will be accompanied by joyous celebration in heaven and on earth. Welcome to this season of hope and expectation!

Jesus himself comes to you. He looks for new ways to touch your heart. He has special gifts for you: reminders of his Father's love, a sense of hope as you face life's challenges, new insights and wisdom that you can share with your loved ones, freedom from guilt as you lay your sins and failings at his feet, and the peace and joy of knowing that you are in the palm of his hand.

Take up God's invitation today! Be alert and ready to receive Jesus and his gifts. Pinpoint things heavy on your heart and spend time in prayer and Scripture reading. Repent of anything that blocks you from receiving God's love and his gifts.

Jesus wants to celebrate with you. Step by step, day by day, you can draw closer to the Lord—and feel him drawing closer to you!

"Jesus, help me get ready to celebrate your coming on Christmas Day and your final coming in glory."

December 14

But now you will be speechless. (Luke 1:20)

Imagine how difficult it must have been for Zechariah to remain silent for nine months. Scripture gives us little insight into this, but we can be sure Zechariah learned patience and trust in God during this period of forced reflection!

In silence we can become aware of our emptiness and our longing for the Lord. While the noise and clutter of the world can dull us spiritually and give us a false sense of fulfillment, silence can dispose us to the Lord, allowing him to fill us and speak to us.

In these days before Christmas, seek the Lord in silence.

Picture Jesus sitting with you, and rest in his presence. God will speak to you. He will bring you peace. He will assure you of his love.

After John was born, Zechariah's "mouth was opened," and he sang God's praises (Luke 1:64). His joy and confidence in the Lord were the fruits of his silence. The same can happen for each of us.

"Lord, help me seek you and find you in the silence of my heart."

December 15

He will . . . turn the hearts of fathers toward children.
(Luke 1:17)

As magical as the season of Christmas is supposed to be, it can also bring the pain of family divisions into stark relief. Whether it's a large gathering of relatives who don't see each other very often, arguments over money, or unreasonably high expectations, divisions that have simmered underground can bubble up and even explode.

It seems that the angel Gabriel had something of this in mind when he told Zechariah that his son, John the Baptist, would "turn the hearts of fathers toward children" (Luke 1:17). And that's exactly what John did. He didn't tell people just to repent to God. He urged them to get right with each other as well. He told those who were well-off to show mercy to the poor by sharing their tunics with them. He told soldiers to stop extorting and falsely accusing the people in their care. And he told tax collectors to stop cheating their fellow citizens.

So who better to ask for help with our families than St. John the Baptist? Ask him to pray with you for any wounded relationship you know of.

"St. John the Baptist, you led many people to Christ through your call to repentance. Pray for me, that I can take steps toward peace and reconciliation as well."

December 16

They shall name him Emmanuel, which means
"God is with us." (Matthew 1:23)

"Emmanuel, God with us." That name must have con-soled Joseph when he woke from his dream. It was like a shield against fear, giving him courage to guard Mary and her child.

Emmanuel: at last, the Messiah whom Israel awaited! God had come to his people in a new and powerful way; he was going to save them from their sins. God kept his promise. He was with them!

This one name—Emmanuel—holds these treasures for you as well. Remember that God is with you, as a friend with whom you can spend each day. Take the time to enjoy that friendship!

He is your courage and strength when you feel unqualified to handle a situation. He is your joy, reminding you of the promise of heaven.

Wrap yourself in the protection of Emmanuel, *God with us*. Rejoice in the truth that God has sent his Son to you. You have a Savior who is always with you!

"Emmanuel, I step forth rejoicing in your faithfulness and in the courage and freedom that you bring to my life."

December 17

Blessed is the fruit of your womb. (Luke 1:42)

The people of the Old Testament were waiting for the Messiah, the one who was going to save them all. They expected a mighty warrior, a wise sage, or a majestic king. But the Messiah came as a little baby.

God came to us in one of the most defenseless ways possible: as a baby. He went through all the stages of growth and came in poverty, showing that every human being, no matter their status, is important to God. He came to embrace every person, including you!

Jesus continued his way of humble vulnerability right up to his death on the cross. He became a beacon, pointing us to how we should model our lives.

Even today, he comes to us in remarkably vulnerable ways: in our fellow Christians, in the poor and needy, in children and the aged. That's how valuable each person is to him!

Jesus stands before you. He invites you to respond to his vulnerability by being vulnerable yourself, by opening your heart and letting him in. Welcome him in his smallness and humility.

"Lord, help me open my heart to you, just as you have opened yours to me."

December 18

*The daybreak from on high will visit us
to shine on those who sit in darkness. (Luke 1:78-79)*

Zechariah speaks for the first time in months, after being struck dumb for doubting the angel's prophecy that he would have a son. Zechariah had always been a godly man, but he seems to have doubted that God would intervene in his life. Now he prophesies, praising God and letting everyone know of the coming Messiah and of his son, John, who will pave the way.

Do you believe that God can work in your life?

He wants to bless you. He wants to show you that he is your heavenly Father and that he cares for you. He wants to give you expectant faith.

Turn to the Lord with hope and expectation.

Ask him for a miracle: for healing for you or someone you love, for the grace to overcome a persistent problem, maybe for something you think is impossible.

God loves seeing his children reach out to him. Let the magnitude of Jesus' birth make you bold and confident.

The Messiah comes to shine on us!

"Jesus, thank you for coming to live among us."

December 19

Stay awake! (Matthew 24:42)

It seems that everywhere you look these days you're being urged to be prepared for something. It could be as practical as your retirement or natural disasters, or as outlandish as Armageddon or the so-called zombie apocalypse. And of course, we need to get ready for the holidays—which is probably a mixture of both the practical and the outlandish!

And yet, amid all the chatter of the season, a quiet, gentle voice invites us, "Prepare the way of the Lord!" (Mark 1:3).

Ready your heart and your mind. Fix your eyes on the child in the manger. Step aside from the onslaught of materialism, and prepare to receive the gifts God has for you.

Your heavenly Father wants to give you peace in the midst of trials. He wants to give you a joy that is based not on fulfilled desires but on his constant presence.

Keep your focus clear as to the "reason for the season"! God loves you completely, warts and all. So make this a time of eager expectation. Talk to God. And listen, for he has good things to say as you prepare to celebrate Jesus' birth.

"Father, I want to receive all that you have for me. Help me stay close to you, to be expectant, and to welcome Jesus into my heart."

December 20

The kingdom of heaven is at hand. (Matthew 10:7)

For thousands of years, faithful Jews awaited the fulfillment of God's promises. They longed for the day when they would "no longer weep" and God would hear their every prayer (Isaiah 30:19). God would sustain them, guide them, and heal their wounds.

Jesus came proclaiming good news: the kingdom has come! He backed up his words with signs and wonders, healing ailing bodies and delivering people from sin and unclean spirits. "His heart was moved with pity for them" (Matthew 9:36).

Yet this was not the Messiah some expected. Many were looking for political rather than spiritual freedom. Of course, God wants us to work against injustice in the world. But true peace and goodness flow out of life in his kingdom.

Let the promise of God's kingdom fill you with hope. And let that promise send you out into the world to make a difference!

How can you be the face of Jesus during this Christmas season?

"Jesus, I want to experience the blessings of your kingdom today. Heal me, feed me, and let your light shine into the dim corners of my heart."

December 21

They were [completely] astounded. (Mark 6:51)

Mark shows us many encounters with Jesus that people found astounding. He freed a man from an unclean spirit at Capernaum (see Mark 1:22), taught in the synagogue of his hometown (see 6:2), and walked across the water to the disciples in their boat. The disciples' "hearts were hardened," or in another translation, "their minds could not grasp" what Jesus had done (6:52, GNT).

Many people still struggle to accept Jesus' words, especially his words about who he is. Some people claim that the Son did not really become human (see 1 John 4:2-3); some, that Jesus was an ethical teacher but not really the Son of God.

The truth of Jesus' incarnation is hard to grasp. We cannot fathom the immortal God becoming a mortal man in order to be close to us and reveal his love to us.

Contemplate the Incarnation. God not only sent his Son but sent him for you! Jesus not only laid down his life but did it out of love for you!

"Jesus, I stand in awe of who you are and all you have done for me."

December 22

Shout with joy to the LORD, all the earth. (Psalm 98:4)

The Bible resounds with the worship of God. From its pages echo the voices of countless men and women, as well as angels, who offer cries and prayers of homage to the Lord. Nature adds its voice to the chorus. Rivers "clap their hands"; mountains "shout with them for joy" (Psalm 98:8).

Many see this psalm as a celebration of the coming of Christ in his incarnation. When the Son of God entered his world, the whole of creation sang. And the joy continues as we await his second coming.

Every human being as well as all of nature have a part to play in this great symphony of praise.

So sing to the Lord! Tell him how much you love him. Let him know how eager you are to see him face-to-face. Tell him how deeply you long for him to come with saving justice and deliver you from all temptation. Invite the created world to join you as you "sing a new song to the LORD" (Psalm 98:1)!

"Lord, I want to join my voice with nature's great symphony of praise to you."

December 23

All were amazed. (Luke 1:63)

You might notice a familiar refrain in the infancy narrative from Luke. Everyone seems to be amazed!

When Zechariah was delayed in the Temple by an angelic visitor, the people waiting for him "were amazed" (Luke 1:21). Here Zechariah's tongue is loosened, and the people are amazed to hear him blessing God. When the shepherds tell the people of Bethlehem of Jesus' birth, they will be "amazed" (2:18). Joseph and Mary will be amazed when Simeon prophesies that their child is the "glory for your people Israel" (2:32).

Jesus is amazing! You have probably seen him work in some amazing ways, and you can trust that he still has a lot of amazing work to do in your life. The promise of Christmas is a promise of new life and new hope; it's a promise that never ends.

Jesus came two thousand years ago, and he still comes to us today. Keep your eyes open and watch for him everyday! He is always with us, no matter what. May we never lose sight of this glorious truth!

"Jesus, fill me with eager expectation as I await your coming on Christmas Day. I believe that you can still amaze me!"

December 24

He has visited and brought redemption to his people.
(Luke 1:68)

Think back to your childhood—to the last long, hot school day before summer holidays started. Recall the anticipation and excitement you felt stepping out of the close, dim classroom into the wide-open sunshine. Every day was filled with possibility and potential.

Christmas Eve can hold the same eager expectancy for you now—but in a quiet, awe-filled sense. It is a day of anticipation, of hope, and of reflection. A day to stop what we're doing and try to spend as much time as possible pondering the light and hope that entered the world when Jesus was born. Jesus came to set us free from sin and to bring us back to our Father's embrace. He came to bring us light in our darkness: the hope of a new life here on earth and the promise of heaven after our days are done.

Jesus' birth was heralded by a star so bright that wise men followed it for hundreds of miles. In Jesus—even in the infant sleeping in the manger—"all the fullness of God [is] pleased to dwell" (Colossians 1:19, NRSV).

Sit quietly today, and ask God to shine his light on you.

"Jesus, thank you for setting me free and shining your light into my life. Teach me how to have it to the full."

December 25

He spoke to us through a son. (Hebrews 1:2)

The sight of a newborn baby melts hearts. The new life is frail and vulnerable, peaceful and beautiful. We can't help but be filled with love.

Jesus, the eternal Word, is the infant of Bethlehem we celebrate today. Here he speaks not in sermons or parables but wordlessly, directly to our hearts. The babe's innocence and vulnerability etch the message of God's grace on our hearts. Jesus reaches out to us and moves us to respond to him, not just with words but with our hearts.

Today is a day of celebrations and family gatherings. It's a day to exchange gifts and wish each other peace and happiness. But it's also a day to gaze at the child in the manger. It's a day for wordless, joyful contemplation.

Savor Jesus' pure, unconditional love for you, and let it bring forth love in you. Reach out and touch him, and let him touch you. Embrace him, and let him hold you close to his heart.

Merry Christmas!

"Here I am, Jesus. Speak, and I will listen."

December 26

*The Word became flesh
and made his dwelling among us. (John 1:14)*

Rather than wait for us to return to him, our holy and unapproachable God—our majestic and all-wise Creator—has come to us!

And we can find him here and now. He jokes at our table. He embraces our relatives. He listens as we express our simplest thanks as well as our deepest desires. We can find him in the innocence of a sleeping baby, the complexity of a snowflake, the surprise of an unplanned encounter, and a line from a familiar carol.

Let us savor God's presence today. This is the key to the Christian life. We can follow the moral code because he walks this road with us. We can love other people because Jesus died for all of us out of love. We can persevere to the end because Jesus went through death to life in a human body like ours.

The Lord of the universe has chosen to make our spaces his permanent dwelling. Let us praise him!

"Father, you created the dignity of human nature and then restored it through your Son. Help us all share in the divinity of Christ."

December 27

They saw the child. (Matthew 2:11)

God manifested his glory to the Magi. They saw a star and chose to follow it all the way to Jesus. They knelt to pay him homage. And the Magi went home changed.

God visits the earth daily. You might say he never left! Every day he stands at the door of your heart and asks, "Can I come in?" (see Revelation 3:20).

Let the divinity of Christ move you to worship. Contemplate who Jesus is and all that he has done for you. Kneel before him—baby in a manger or Savior on a cross—and let joy and gratitude fill you, just as the Magi experienced.

Imagine how it was for the Magi to go home and return to their normal lives. Truly they arrived there "by another way" (Matthew 2:21). They had seen the glory of God, and nothing would be the same again!

Your life can be changed too as you see Jesus, worship him, and receive new insights from the Spirit.

"Lord, help me see you anew."

December 28

They opened their treasures and offered him gifts.
(Matthew 2:11)

The Magi gave the infant Jesus gifts of gold, frankincense, and myrrh. These gifts had symbolic value and were probably helpful as well during the family's flight into Egypt.

We have the opportunity to offer the Lord gifts of our own. What gift can we possibly offer the Creator and Lord of the universe?

A verse from the poet Christina Rossetti has it right: "What can I give Him, poor as I am? . . . give my heart."

God is delighted when we offer him what no one else can give: ourselves. No one can praise God the same way as you. No one can follow him down the same path. No one but you can love the set of people he has given you to love, with the particular gifts he has given you.

Let us give Jesus ourselves, a gift that fills him with delight.

"Lord Jesus, I give you my heart, the heart you created to love you."

December 29

My eyes have seen your salvation. (Luke 2:30)

While Simeon had a specific role in announcing God's plan of salvation, he didn't have a script or instruction manual, let alone a calendar to tell him the day and place of the announcement.

Rather, he was prepared through waiting—in hope, trust, and confidence—for God to accomplish what he had promised.

What a model for our lives! We too are called to announce God's plan of salvation to those close to us. Maybe not as dramatically as Simeon did, or even as specifically—but then again, maybe so! Either way, we can be prepared, as Simeon was, by knowing God's word, pondering it, and being confident in what God says.

Does this sound like too big a job for you? It's not, really. Start simply by quieting your heart before God and asking him to fill it. Ask him for a sense of his love, and allow Jesus to perfect it in you (see 1 John 2:5).

Try your best to obey what you know God is asking you to do, and you will find the love and presence of God spilling out of you to all the people in your life.

"Father, I open my heart to you. Fill me with your love today. Give me more and more of it until it brims over in me and runs out to others."

December 30

[John the Baptist] saw Jesus coming toward him.
(John 1:29)

From his mother's womb, John the Baptist recognized Jesus' presence (see Luke 1:41-44). As a prophet living in the desert, he testified to the coming Messiah and called people to repentance. Jesus was so impressed with John's keen vision that he said, "Among those born of women there has been none greater than John the Baptist" (Matthew 11:11).

But John didn't recognize Jesus on his own. The Spirit opened his eyes so that he could say, "Now I have seen and testified that he is the Son of God" (John 1:34).

God is working everywhere. Jesus is always "coming toward" us with his grace and his blessing, inviting us to share that grace with the people around us.

So ask the Holy Spirit to open your eyes today so that you can see Jesus. You might be surprised by what he shows you.

And don't worry if you don't see anything right away. Simply asking the Spirit for this grace is a sign that Jesus is at work in you.

"Holy Spirit, help me see Jesus and share him with the people around me."

December 31

Can the wedding guests fast while the bridegroom is with them? (Mark 2:19)

Jesus wasn't the kind of Messiah most people expected. He came as a humble, poor rabbi. And he came as a friend and even bridegroom, to love his people into new life.

Jesus came to lay down his life for his people, as an honorable husband would do for his wife. He came to teach forgiveness, a teaching he would embody as he hung on the cross, praying, "Father, forgive them" (Luke 23:34).

Jesus is the Messiah. Perhaps we picture him up in heaven, removed from our circumstances. Or we focus on his moral teachings and forget about his power to change lives. Jesus isn't removed; he's close to us all the time. And he isn't just a teacher; he is almighty God.

Jesus stands by our side, ready to lift us up with his love. Even when we sin, he is with us, offering his healing and calling us back to himself in love.

Over the past 365 days, he has offered us healing and has called us back to himself in love. As the new year approaches, let us remember that Jesus stands by our side, ready to lift us up with his love. He truly is our Bridegroom!

"Jesus, reveal yourself to me today. You are my hope!"

Notes

Complete Catholic Mass and Daily Meditations

the WORD among us
DAILY MEDITATIONS FOR CATHOLICS

SEPTEMBER 2020
WAU.ORG

Be Holy, For I the Lord Am Holy

WHAT DOES HOLINESS LOOK LIKE TODAY?

Sharing the Love of CHRIST

The Heart of a Missionary Disciple

Evangelization. The word can make us feel uncomfortable and apprehensive. As Christians, we know that we should be sharing the good news. But it's easy to think that it's a calling for others—missionaries, religious, those in lay ministry. After all, they know more than we do about the faith, and they have the proper training. Where would we even begin?

It's not as difficult as you might think. In this issue, John and Therese Boucher outline four simple steps that anyone can do to share their faith: praying, caring, sharing faith in conversations, and daring to invite others into a faith-filled community. The Bouchers are authors and teachers who have been involved in Church evangelization efforts for many years. We hope their time-tested wisdom, adapted from their book *Sharing the Faith That You Love*, will help spark a greater desire to share your faith and encourage you to become confident in your ability to do so. ✦

God's invitation to share your faith may have begun with a growing concern about your adult children or about nieces and nephews who don't go to church. Perhaps God is speaking to you through the sparse